Confessions
of a
Call Centre Worker

Izabelle Winter

Dragontale Publishers, Cardiff

ISBN-13:978-1539390992

Dedication

This book is dedicated to all my former colleagues and those still incarcerated in call centres, especially Andrea, Leeky Lee, Sue, Esther and Marie.
May the force be with you.

For the time being and forever, I'm out!

Contents

Looking For a New Career?

Are you looking for a change of career? Do you fancy a nice cushy job where you can sit in a refreshing, air conditioned office, in a comfy chair with free tea and coffee, lots of mates around to talk to, with abundant office gossip, fun and supportive managers?

Does the idea of chatting to lovely people on the phone all day, helping them with their queries and then mutually wishing each other a lovely day at the end of the call appeal to you?

Do you want to come to work, do your job then leave on time with a sense of fulfilment?

Are you the type who'd like to leap out of bed full of the joys of spring on a Monday morning, shouting 'Oh Boy! I love my job'?

You are? Then a call centre is not for you.

Quotes from ex-colleagues:

Gareth; "I'd prefer to staple my bollocks to a raging bull and ride it through a minefield than work in another call centre."

Jo: "That headset sucked the very essence from my soul. Like a cow plugged into a milking machine, all my charisma, enthusiasm for life, joie de vivre and my mojo, call by call, all gone forever. I'll never be the same again."

Eloise: "Don't do it. Just don't."

Hev: "Call Centre… (the rest wasn't publishable).

Introduction

Over the past thirty or so years, I've worked in several different call centres; each as different in its own way as the company it represented. Whatever the company, in whatever industry, I found communicating with the public over the telephone was very similar.

Each centre had a huge range of wild and wacky characters as well as one or two fairly ordinary people. Each with their own reasons for working there; most, because they needed an income, some as a stop-gap while studying for a degree, others because they needed the unsociable hours to juggle the needs of a family. For a few it was a second job and one man even worked there because he liked it. I've never met anyone who left school with the sole ambition of working in a call centre.

Whatever our background, once we'd signed on the dotted line and plugged in to the phones, we were all colleagues together. The customer on the other end of the line had no idea who they were talking to or where the staff member was based and most of the time they really didn't care.

As the staff were individuals, so were the customers: a few were sweet and charming, others were somewhat challenging, occasionally they called direct from Hell.

Customers had no idea if they'd be talking to a seasoned professional, a student on his first job, a worker in another continent or a manager helping out during a busy spell.

Customers regularly spoke to us as if we were something which had just been scraped off their shoe.

Mr and Mrs Public appeared to think call centre operators were fair game for as much abuse as they wished to spew forth until they felt relieved of whatever pent up stress they'd accumulated over the preceding hour/day/month/year. Some folk treated us as if we were amoebas with the intellectual ability of ant dandruff lying at the very bottom of the barrel of life. Even so, we were heavily discouraged from following the urge to advise the caller to stick their attitude where the sun didn't shine.

A colleague who had two jobs to make ends meet at home was told by a customer, 'I know you unfortunates can only dream of earning what I earn and I really don't have time to be messing about with you people on the phone'.

An Asian colleague at the next desk, who'd lived in the UK since he was two, was told by a customer, 'I don't want to talk to you; I want to talk to someone in my own country'.

Another was told, 'I want to speak to someone who earns more money than you.' He resisted the urge to reply 'well you can speak to the Queen if you have her number, but she's not going to help you with your query is she?'

We were there to help. Whatever it was our employer had or hadn't done, wasn't personally our fault; even so, we always tried to do our utmost to find a solution. We knew what could be done and the appropriate action to take. We actually wanted to make customers happy; after all, if the customer was happy then they wouldn't scream at us.

If you've never had the unique experience of working in a call centre, I'll try to enlighten you. Although, as

4

much as I grumbled along with everybody else, whenever I managed to escape the clutches of one, I always seemed to find myself gravitating back to another.

It's not my intention to put you off if you're determined on a call centre career, although this book is intended as a bit of light relief for the long-suffering souls already there. Please read, enjoy and know you are never alone.

I hope you'll find humour in the familiar and read this in the light-hearted manner in which it was intended. Names, places and company names have all been changed to protect the innocent and the not so innocent.

All calls are real or based on real events, some may have been altered slightly for the sake of anonymity. This book is not a manual or a how-to but merely my own observations over 25 years of working in call centres.

1. Can't Take Any More

Sunday morning 03:07; the more I re-arranged my bedclothes, turned my pillow, opened the window, and checked my phone, the more awake I became. Further exaggerated pillow-fiddling, deep breathing followed by counting herds of sheep and a lot of swearing didn't help either.

I battled my inner demons to get back to sleep and they fought back with snippets of call centre conversations I'd had with customers over previous weeks. Some were simple or mundane queries with little more than a yes or no answer required; others had been far more challenging. One or two made jumping out of the window seem appealing even though we were on the fourth floor. Others were so ridiculous it was laughable, especially when some people waited over thirty minutes on the phone to ask them.

I was still awake at 03:47, not because the weekend had been particularly exciting, but because the Friday afternoon at work had been memorably bad. We'd had the usual mix of calls from hell and the thought of returning to take more of them on Monday morning hung over me like a cloud of doom.

Nothing would allow me to drop off into the land of zeds, so I resorted to my trusted method of writing a list. I've always been a list person; places to visit before I die, chores to be done before Christmas, things I'd like to learn, places I'd like to visit; any list would do, I just needed a subject…

Moments later the ink began to flow;

Title: **'*Reasons not to go to work on Monday*'.**

1) I don't want to go.
2) Call-centres give me a headache.
3) Telephones give me a headache.
4) Customers give me a headache.
5) The headset makes my ears itch.
6) The office is often too hot.
7) The office is often too cold.
8) I don't like the 'Big Brother' atmosphere.
9) My team colleagues are half my age.
10) My manager is half my age.

Ten reasons without pausing for breath and there were lots more;

11) I need a more fulfilling job.
12) My stomach ties itself in knots the moment I walk through the door.
13) I rarely get out on time if I'm stuck on a call.
14) I rarely get to break on time.
15) I don't like the coffee.
16) Sitting at the desk all day gives me backache.
17) Office politics are like being in infant school.
18) My confidence is taking a pounding.
19) I need a job I enjoy and want to get up for.
20) I deserve a job I enjoy. Hey! I'm worth it!

I was on a roll and my intention was merely to fall asleep from list-writing boredom, so I kept going.

21) Friends have *their* dream jobs so I want mine.
22) My kids are calling me a grumpy old moo.
23) My husband is calling me a grumpy old moo.
24) My friends call me a grumpy old moo.
25) I must be a grumpy old moo.

Much as I hated to admit it, I often came home from work in a very bad mood and remained that way until I somehow got the day out of my head. My family didn't really give a stuff about listening to my whinges.

26) Despite almost two years in the same office I have no close friends.
27) Nobody knows the real me.
28) I barely know anybody properly.
29) There has to be more to life than this.
30) Not once in two years have I ever been to lunch with anybody from the office.

The items on my list were all only slight variations on a theme but I was already getting sleepy, so I carried on;

31) The wages are rubbish.
32) The office is too far from home.
33) The car parking is rubbish.
34) There's nowhere safe to park my bike.
35) I rarely get the holiday dates I want.
36) The office stinks of feet.
37) A few staff stink of stale fags and wet-dog.
38) The coffee machine is always broken.

39) If I have to listen to Pete clicking his false teeth all day long for much longer I will not be responsible for my actions.

40) The canteen microwave is a health hazard and should be condemned.

Some of the reasons were silly, nevertheless they were valid to me and so I wrote them down.

At 07:29 I woke up again with the light still on, the list on the floor and an interesting pen-shaped indent on my left cheek.

I wandered downstairs, list in hand and read over it while I put the kettle on for a strong coffee.

The final total of fifty-nine reasons made it sound like the worst job in the world. Did I really hate it that much?

On good days at least it was dry and sometimes even warm. We were allowed to wear whatever we liked, within reason and could have drinks at our desks. Most staff were lovely and the office buzz was positive. We worked as one team, all facing the same issues together. Occasionally, when the phones were quiet we even had a bit of a laugh. We regularly shared sweets and cakes and got coffee for each other. We all chipped in when someone had a birthday, wedding or a baby and we congratulated those who left, albeit with a sense of jealousy.

There was a lot to gossip about and with the high staff turnover there were always new staff members to welcome to the fold. Occasionally even the customers were a delight and brightened our day. Very occasionally the whole day was wonderful from start to finish.

Unfortunately, unless staff socialised outside

work, nobody ever really got to know each other properly. Once plugged in to the phones and attached to our desks by the hotwire to hell, any in-depth conversations off the phones were out of the question. We were barely able to squeeze a word in.

Our time was monitored to the second. We were occasionally briefly able to speak to colleagues at the coffee machine or exchange a quick 'Hi' in passing. Despite colleagues sitting only a few desks away, we often didn't even know each other's names.

A chat at the fax or photocopier was out of the question in some places because these machines were for people far above lowly call handlers to use. Time at the fax machine was time away from the phones so using them was discouraged.

I read the rest of the reasons on my list;

41) I fancy a few weeks off.
42) I'll have time to look for a better job.
43) I always feel stressed.
44) I feel constantly under pressure.
45) It's best to leave while the going is good.
46) If I don't leave soon, I may well snap and do something regrettable.
47) My PC monitor is temperamental.
48) The 'N' on my keyboard keeps falling off.
49) My mouse keeps sticking.
50) I feel jealous of people who work elsewhere.
51) I can't stand being near Frank. (Frank was an annoyingly patronising old git, who'd worked in the same job forever and believed he knew everything. He answered colleagues' queries

very reluctantly, unless the colleague was female, young and gorgeous. Often his replies were merely a very loud, 'You should know that!' making the asker feel humiliated and put off asking him anything ever again.)

52) There's no time to for reading important emails, (meant to be read, absorbed and actioned in between calls) because it's always busy.

53) There's also no time to do training or staff appraisal preparation in between calls.

54) I haven't gone home on time in over three weeks.

55) I don't like the schoolroom atmosphere.

56) I get a headache the minute I walk in the door which goes the minute I walk out.

57) The call centre diet is unhealthy; my butt is expanding daily, along with my stomach and tally of chins.

58) The air-conditioning, when it works, spreads diseases faster than the black-death.

59) The keyboards are equally risky.

As I sat there mulling over my list, my husband appeared, clearly unimpressed I'd not made the coffee yet. 'What's that? No, let me guess; another list?' He's used to me making lists, I guess it's one of my many lovable little quirks.

'It's my "*Reasons not to go to work on Monday morning*," list.'

'Oh, this is gonna be a good one; go on how many?'

'Fifty-nine.'

'Fifty-nine?' He looked at me stunned as he bit

into his toast and chewed it thoughtfully while butter ran down his chin. 'Why the hell are you going in then?'

Why *was* I going to work? It was a valid point. Surely my sanity was worth far more than a few weeks' wages? How hard could it be to get another job, anything, even if it was shelf-filling in a supermarket? Any job which didn't involve answering telephones had to be a better option.

I had also noticed a disturbing habit I had acquired where each time I took a difficult call I started scratching my head and pulling out chunks of hair. My colleagues had also noticed it.

At the wrong side of forty, perhaps I should have become a high-flying career woman in a decent job, or at least be somewhere I enjoyed working. Yet there I was, still at the bottom of the career ladder with no ambition whatsoever to climb any higher with the current company. I was just one of millions of other call centre workers in the world and I hated every single minute.

Since I loathed it so much, something had to change. If I didn't have my career-for-life by the time I was fifty, then I figured I may as well give up and resign myself to being a call centre worker for the rest of my sorry working life. What I needed was a 'proper job'. Whatever that meant, I knew it wouldn't be in a call centre.

The following day, Monday morning at 09:00 I walked into work, knowing I didn't want to be there yet still unsure whether I had the balls to do anything about it. If I did, what should I do and when should I do it?

The callboard brought me back to reality.

There were already 59 calls waiting, the same number of reasons on my list. Something in my head clicked.

I went through the motions of logging on, did a brief check of my emails and jammed my headset over my ears. Feeling the familiar knot tying itself in my stomach I glanced outside the window: the early morning sunlight danced onto my desk through the trees in the car park, tempting me outside. I could just see the sky through a distant window; a deep, cloudless blue with the promise of a lazy, warm day.

My team-mates were already logged in. Pete at the desk next to mine was taking his first call 'Good Morning, you're through to Pete. How can I help?' He clicked his teeth, 'I see, you want to make a complaint, OK, let me just...' he rolled his eyes at me. Good old Monday morning.

Every inch of me wanted to be somewhere else, anywhere else. I signed in and with a deep sigh, clicked my *ready* button. Immediately the beep sounded and I went into autopilot.

'Good Morning, thank you for calling, my name's Izzy, How may I...'

'I've been hangin' on this god-damn bloody phone fifteen minutes, it's absolutely ridiculous. If you think you're going to...'

If I needed a final nail in the coffin of my call centre life, that was it. With a simple click of the mouse on the magic *end-call* button, the caller disappeared. I knew from that very moment I could never take another call in a call centre again.

I walked over to speak with my manager and asked to have a few words in private. I explained about my list and that it had merely served to confirm what my mind had been telling me for a long time, a call centre was not for me and I couldn't stand the job a minute longer. He understood completely.

Ten minutes later, bag and coat in hand, I walked out, past the callboard showing a seething queue of 27 calls waiting. I had the widest grin on my face as I left my call centre life behind forever.

So long suckers. I felt epic.

The early April sunshine warmed my back and there was a fresh spring in my step. The knot which had been in my stomach for months, slowly untied and I had to pinch myself to make sure it was real. All the pressure of the past months and years lifted. I was free. I walked to my car almost skipping as I went and drove home performing in-car karaoke loudly all the way home.

2. Where it all Began

Did I do the right thing? Hell yeah! I have no doubt I will never work in a call centre again.

You may like the idea though... Perhaps you should decide after I've shared some of the highs and lows of the job. I'll share some of the conversations I've had with customers and some of the everyday workings of a call centre with lots more besides.

I left school all those years ago with ten GCSEs but no clear idea of the career I wanted to follow. While most of my friends headed off to college or university, I didn't even know which industry I wanted to go into. I spent another two years studying a BTEC National Business Diploma to give me more time to make up my mind. That was, I suspect, the start of the slippery slope towards the call centre.

In the beginning it wasn't all doom and gloom. There were a few good parts. Some staff loved to talk to customers all day and enjoyed the challenge of turning a furious customer around by sorting out their issues for them.

Occasionally, during a late shift or if there was a quiet moment it was possible to find out a bit about other colleagues. It sometimes felt like another family with team members looking out for each other. There was always plenty of gossip and the general atmosphere between staff was good.

After college I took a cashier job with a building society for a year and my future looked bright. However, shortly after that I split up with a loser boyfriend and needed time to get myself back on track.

Not one to do things by halves, I left not only the cashier job but also the UK to work in a ski resort in France for a season as one of a team of twelve hotel assistants. Our job was to look after the hotel public areas and give the rooms a quick spruce each day. We also had a rota for serving breakfast and evening meals to the clients. We could ski from midday until the lifts closed every day except Friday, when old guests left and new ones arrived. The health benefits were amazing and the only stress was when the rooms weren't clean in time for the guests' arrival or when a bowl of fries needed a refill at dinner.

The same year I worked as an office assistant for Camp America, spending all summer in a quaint wooden log cabin in Camp Kennebec overlooking Salmon Lake in Maine, USA. The camp I was on was a typical American residential camp where boys came from all over the country to spend their summer learning new skills and activities.

Maine remains one of my favourite places ever. I love how the seasons are defined and it's possible to ski there in the winter and swim outside in a lake just miles away in the summer.

I was having such a blast back then that instead of taking one year out, I took three, alternating winters in ski resorts in France with summers in America. Although by my third year working away, most of my friends from school were either married with families or settled in a career, steadily climbing their way to the top, I have no regrets. It wasn't until I hit the grand age of 24, I decided I should finally settle down to a 'proper job'.

Within four weeks of my return to the UK, I took a job in my very first call centre, making calls to local businesses to try to persuade them to place an advertisement in the local free newspaper.

Sitting in a chair all day, chatting on the phone and getting paid as well; it sounded charming. What was there not to like about a job like that?

I soon found out.

Initially there were three weeks in the classroom learning selling techniques. We were taught how to get through to the person who made the decisions by asking for them by their first name and acting like we'd known them for years. We were shown how to deal with any negativity and how to become the customer's friend.

There was a whole list of possible negative points they may have said and a list of answers for each one.

They drummed into us we should never assume anything. 'ASSUME - makes an ASS of U and ME,' was written on the flip chart and was given as one of many handouts to pin on our desks.

We learned how to really listen to the customer and to make notes for future conversations so each customer honestly believed we cared about their cat's in-growing toenail or their blocked U-bend. Each customer was to be made to feel special and as if the offer being made was the best ever and they really needed it.

We were told to suggest the price the customer was initially offered could possibly be lowered as they were such a good, new, old, returning or special customer. We weren't allowed to call anyone on current customer lists as these 'belonged' to the most senior staff. We were given the yellow pages and other local papers to find our own customers; this was long before the internet.

The office was on the fourth floor of a dreary old and grey concrete building. The lift never worked the whole time I worked there. It wasn't the sort of place any decent individual would want to go after dark. The whole place stank of stale urine from the old tramps who hung about in the doorway.

The office heating was either full on or full off. In summer there was a single battered old fan at the front of the office which couldn't be used; it was noisy and blew the paperwork all round the room and occasionally out of the windows. The building was pre-war and had been earmarked for demolition as part of the city regeneration plan, so there was never any possibility of air conditioning being installed. In the summer we all baked and in the winter we froze.

As appears to be the norm in such offices, the windows were screwed shut, all apart from one which was broken and rattled in the wind. If some optimistic soul propped it open in a vain quest for air it was almost always immediately shut again; even on the fourth floor, the noise from outside was too loud to hear the customers on the telephones.

The desks were set out in rows facing the manager; he watched us from an elevated platform behind a large table. Behind him was a huge white-board; whenever someone made a sale they shouted out and had a running total added to their name for all to see. This also meant that anyone who had made no sales was glaringly obvious. That person was usually me.

The walls were stained yellow with nicotine from the staffroom just inside the main doors. At the time smoking was still allowed inside and nobody dared to complain; most of the staff were chain-smokers anyway. Nobody seemed concerned that we all spent our break-times contracting lung disease. The staff room windows were also screwed shut, which seemed somewhat unnecessary on the fourth floor, although it removed the temptation to leap to freedom.

Outbound cold calls were the ones most customers hated receiving, usually because they were busy doing something else; in the middle of dinner, putting the kids to bed, catching some sneaky z's, about to go out, rushing to get to work or just relaxing in their own house. People immediately became defensive because they believed the caller was either trying to sell them something or trying to do a survey. They were usually right.

From the worker's point of view, this job required a persuasive, charismatic personality, bags of stamina, and the ability to retain the will to live against all odds. Together with each outgoing call went a tiny piece of their soul…

Our first challenge was actually getting hold of the right person. If we managed to get any sort of reply at all it was usually one of the following;

'Sorry they moved away years ago.'
'Not interested.'
'Whatever you're selling we've already got one.'
'Sorry, he died.'
'She's out.'
'What d'ya mean is Mummy in? I *am* Mummy.'
'Go f*** yourself.'

Some call centres used an automated system where a member of staff was only allocated the call once it was answered, and only then were they informed who they'd 'called'. These automated systems caused 'silent' calls which so infuriated customers; especially after they'd tripped over the cat and spilled their coffee rushing to answer the phone.

When I was younger those silent calls worried my parents because back then it potentially meant that someone was calling the house to see when the occupants were out with the intention of breaking in. Nowadays it usually means that the call centre have got their figures wrong and dialed more calls than they have staff to deal with. It still worries some elderly people.

As a customer, I hate receiving unwanted calls, especially from someone speaking in a very strong, often unintelligible foreign accent, usually trying to sell me something I don't want under the flimsy disguise of doing a 'quick survey'.

The call usually starts with a 'Hello Ma'am' which in itself is almost guaranteed not to be a caller from the UK. We don't use that term over here and personally I hate being called 'Ma'am' as it makes me sound like some old school mistress. They then ask if I am the 'lady of the house,' again, highly suspicious. What then follows is a scripted cheery introduction where they pretend to care whether I am having a good day.

'How are you today?'

'I'm fine thank you.'

'Oh, very good Ma'am. I am so very pleased to hear you are having a good day. Don't worry; I'm not trying to sell you anything.' This is a distortion of the truth, I know it and they know it. They're on a *fishing* mission so they can pass my details to someone who *will* call back and try to sell me something.

Then lie number two; 'I'm calling with a very short survey...' This translates to 'I will keep asking you questions about anything and everything until you either hang up or lose the will to live.'

Up to this point it's best to be polite, just in case it really is Camelot calling you regarding a lottery win.

Most likely it's not either of these so the best tactic as a customer is probably to politely refuse and hang up. Anybody drawn into a conversation, or worse who hands over money, is put on a S*uckers List* for life.

Knowing how much many people hated receiving these calls, it was surprising I ever managed to pick up the nerve to make them myself. Back then I was young and lived at home where my parents answered most of the calls. Even so, I'm sure they never had half the amount I currently receive.

This was the point in my career I was first introduced to the headset, a beastly form of torture designed to be worn all day. It's a cross between a set of child's comic ears and a prop from *Dr. Who.*

The training films regularly hammered home that this evil head extension was a highly expensive piece of 'state of the art' technology. Even so, as newbies we were given a stone-age version which weighed a ton and smelled like rancid feet. The thing caused itchy ears and launched itself onto the floor at the most inappropriate moments and often if the wearer dared to move more than a foot from their workstation. The wire shackling us to the lines from hell was often responsible for spilling coffee all over the desk and for many near-death experiences from strangulation after becoming tangled around the arm of the chair.

According to the training film it could be styled around the hair and was designed to be worn in perfect comfort all day. It merely had to be unclipped with the mouthpiece raised above the head when not required.

In reality the mouthpiece would be loose and would drop just as the wearer attempted to sneak a sip of boiling coffee flavoured drink from the office machine. The coffee and tea tasted identical and were so full of cleaning chemicals I'm surprised Health and Safety hadn't intervened.

Armed with the Devil's headband and all the enthusiasm of a young newbie, I did as I was told and began to call as many businesses as I could find, being careful not to tread on any of my colleague's toes by calling 'their' companies.

Time after time, after time, the response was;

'Not Interested.'

'Maybe next month.'

'Just leave us alone.'

'Not you people again.'

'I wouldn't advertise with you if you were the last paper on earth.'

'Not after you cocked up the last one.'

'You've got to be effing joking!'

With each new call my enthusiasm died a little and in no time at all I was starting to sound less like the smiley happy voiced person they had encouraged in training and more like a suicidal zombie.

Other customer responses included;

'Leave me alone my dog just died.'

'If you lot call me again I'll come round there and personally beat the **** out of you.'

'Haven't you got anything better to do?'

I learned, pretty fast, that tele-marketing was a dog-eat-dog world where rules were rules except when those brave enough to do so, broke them.

Whether I was allowed to break the rules depended on; the manager's mood, the office temperature, whether it was a big or a small rule, whether it made money for the company, who was breaking it and how close to the publishing deadline it was.

Some rules could only be bent by certain people and broken only in certain circumstances.

I had the biggest ad I ever booked stolen from me by the person who was supposed to be my mentor. His reasoning was that as I wasn't going to hit my target anyway I had nothing to lose, whereas my booking would make him seller of the month and win him a prize. If ever the scenario was reversed, he said, he'd return the favour. Stupidly I let him get away with it.

One deadline day, after a whole week of no sales, I had a customer who asked 'Can you call me back later?' With a great sense of relief I saw this as a lead and a potential sale to save my back; like a drowning woman with a straw. I dutifully rang back two hours later.

The same woman answered 'Can you call back later, I'm making lunch?'

Hey no problem, she probably had kids to feed. It seemed she was clearly interested.

Two hours after that I rang again.

'I need to think about it. Can you call back?'

I thought perhaps she needed to decide the wording for the ad, surely a positive thing, no problem, I'd call again just before I went home. With all the negativity from other customers at least I had this lead to fall back on.

I rang again just before my shift ended.

'Good afternoon, it's…'

'For God's sake don't you get the damn message,' she screamed. 'I'm NOT INTERESTED!'

I was taken aback anyone would act that way towards me or speak to me like that. Clearly I had a lot to learn. I screamed back, 'Well why didn't you just say that instead of wasting my time?' I was furious and hung up on her. She'd been stringing me along all day, pointlessly and giving me hope when she'd clearly had no intention of taking out an ad.

Why the heck didn't she say that on my first call? The wretched woman then had the gall to call back and complain about me and my attitude. My manager told me to call her back to apologise. I refused and so that was the end of that job.

3. The Inbound Centre

Not learning from my dismal experience in the first dreary hell-hole, I managed to get another job with another newspaper, the local daily.

This time I had to cold-call members of the public at home in the evenings and offer them various incentives to have their paper delivered every day for a month. To be fair the offer wasn't bad, a free paper for two weeks, free delivery and a coffee-maker/deep fat fryer or whatever the current offer was. We were paid £2 a sale plus the minimum wage.

We were each given a few pages, ripped from the telephone directory and told to plough through, picking up different areas of the city each time. Some of the directories were years old and the numbers had since been made ex-directory. Many people didn't like being called at home and some were highly suspicious.

They'd demand 'Where did you get my number?'

'Er. It was in the phone book.'

Then they'd continue with a tirade of how their number wasn't in the phone book anymore and this made them highly suspicious.

They'd ramble on and on about how they had specifically asked to be ex-directory and therefore I *had* to be lying. This would lead to an argument of how I got their number and which phone book my page came from and on and on until they demanded to speak to my manager. Clearly this was wasting everybody's time. We hadn't even got to the reason for calling at that point.

The most frustrating reason customers gave

for not wanting the paper delivered was that they liked to go to the shop themselves and walk the dog at the same time. I pointed out that delivery would mean they could walk their dog to the park instead and if it rained they didn't have to get wet.

I'm sure all the reasons given were probably just excuses because people never like to be called at home by someone trying to sell them something. People were wary of cold callers and believed if something sounded too good to be true, it probably was.

When people were at home they weren't in the right frame of mind to try to work out the catch and therefore they felt saying no was their best option.

That job only lasted about three weeks, by which time I could take no more. It was time to re-evaluate my career. Clearly outbound call-centres were not for me.

Just two weeks later I secured myself a new job, this time in an inbound call centre. I assumed this would surely be better than an outbound one because the customers made the call when it was convenient for them and they wanted to speak to someone. This should make them slightly more amenable. It sounded easy; they called, I'd help them, they'd thank me politely and go.

How wrong I was.

I was initially extremely enthusiastic about the new job. The offices were freshly decorated with air conditioning and heating which actually worked. There was even a proper break room with an on-site canteen.

This job was with a motor insurance company

based in the city centre. I felt I'd moved onwards and upwards. An LED board on the wall scrolled a message in red and green lights. 'WELCOME TO INSUREYOURSELF... HAVE A GREAT DAY...'

How very thoughtful. In my mind I pictured the board relaying messages and updates throughout the day with perhaps a spot of news or the odd birthday greeting. I soon discovered this was a call-board and quickly learned the thing was utterly evil.

My job appeared to be fairly simple; I had to ask the customers a set of questions which were listed on the PC screen; once these had been answered I was able to provide the caller with the price for a year's car insurance. If the customer accepted the policy I'd take the payment details and issue the documents. There were also extras which could be offered with a cash incentive for each sale.

We had the standard introduction talk with a film about how the headset was our friend and a very hi-tech and expensive piece of equipment. It was to be looked after, not lent to anyone and locked away when not in use.

I was pleasantly surprised when we were each issued with a shiny, brand new headset, still in its original individual box with a little black protector bag inside and a spare ear pad.

We were each introduced to a *buddy* to sit with on our first day. This was a current member of staff who would answer all our questions.

My buddy was Lucy, a young, bubbly, chatty girl who apparently oozed confidence and passion for the company. This was her first job since leaving school and so far she loved it. She said the company was wonderful, the job was 'fab' and the atmosphere was 'totally amazing'. She told me she felt valued and carried on gushing about what a great company it was.

I wondered whether she'd been briefed on what to say to the newbies so I asked how long she'd been in the job.

'Five weeks,' she replied.

Like many other call centres, this one was huge, employing hundreds of people. It was a massive hive of activity where staff sat behind rows upon rows of desks, packed in like battery hens. The calls were mainly from UK based customers although the caller could be from anywhere in the world.

As a call taker, we had no idea who the next caller may be; sweet old lady or total psycho. Whoever it was we were expected to treat them all with professionalism and politely deal with whatever they verbally threw at us.

When a call came through, it was introduced by way of a loud '*BEEEEP*!' This was a type of safety shutdown valve making sure nothing inappropriate would reach the customer's delicate ears. It meant; *Stop all office conversation immediately, forget any punch lines and you may as well abandon all hope of any meaningful conversation with your colleagues, ever.*

I can think of no other job on earth where people can sit less than three metres away from another colleague for months on end and never get the chance to get to know them. This is because most of their time is spent chatting over a thin telephone wire to someone miles away who they'd probably never met and thankfully, in most cases, were never likely to meet.

The only time I got to have a real conversation with my colleagues was when the phones crashed or during a monthly meeting. Those were moments to be cherished.

If we bumped into somebody in the corridor or by the coffee machine we could chat briefly, but time was precious. Aside from official tea breaks there was a daily limit of just eight minutes 'comfort break' to take time out for a quick ciggie, a drink, visit the ladies' room or anything else we needed. Time was monitored to the second.

The initial training for the inbound call centre was about three to four weeks although they gave regular updates during the year. We had training sessions and films on almost everything.

1) Health and Safety
2) The Company History
3) Fire Safety
4) The Company Procedures, Codes and Mottos
5) How to use your PC and Phone System
6) Data Protection
7) Fraud Awareness and Money Laundering
8) Bullying Awareness
9) Manual Handling
10) Your Workstation
11) Emergency Drill
12) Complaint Handling
13) Customers and Communications

Most of the training was common sense and deathly boring. The trainees knew it, the company knew it, but it still had to be done.

The customer communication film informed us we should always smile during the call so that we sounded friendlier. Smiling gave better results as the customer would pick up they were speaking to a nice, happy and friendly person and so be nicer to us and apparently then buy our product as a result. Think of baby advertisements on TV and you'll know what I mean. In my opinion being too happy sounded sarcastic; clearly I had a lot to learn.

If the customer wanted to complain, we were told to let them vent and get whatever it was off their chest. If they wanted to ramble on about something, so be it. Once the wind was out of their sails then we could jump in with our fabulous helpful attitude and complaint-sorting abilities and amaze them; at least that's how it worked in training.

They also told us to never assume anything and always listen attentively to the customer. We were to try to personalise the call; 'That sounds like a big dog you have there, what's his name?' or 'Oh dear, junior doesn't sound too happy,' when a child was screeching at full volume next to the phone.

The standard company greeting was to be given on every call followed by our name and then 'How may I help you?' We were always to give the current customer 100% of our attention, and ignore the callboard when it showed there were many more calls waiting...

In conclusion, we had to ask, 'Is there anything else I can help you with?' on every single call.

Training was one thing but actually speaking to real members of the public was another thing altogether and I soon learned there were as many levels of stupid as there were customers and they never ceased to amaze me.

When, three weeks later I was fully trained and met my new team leader, he told me "ignore everything you've learned in training; it's total bollocks; This is the real world." And so it was.

In the real world, once the customer had vented, they'd vent some more; then they'd repeat the foregoing vent even louder and when I attempted to help, they'd demand a manager.

If a customer swore, we were told to say something like "Sir, I must warn you, if you use that language again I'll have to terminate the call." All call operators hoped and prayed that the customer *did* swear again because then they could use the red button to end the call which was one of the most satisfying parts of the job.

Whether it was sorted immediately or by the promise of a call back, the customer always had to hang up first. This was a total pain if a customer wasn't happy, because at the end of the call asking 'Is there anything else I can help you with?' was like holding the proverbial can of worms and handing the can opener to the customer.

Despite greeting the customer with my full name at the start of each call, most of them would have forgotten it only seconds later. The only exception was when a customer wanted a name so they could shout at someone. In those cases they would use my name as a verbal punch bag to pepper sentences with. 'So, Izzy, you think I'm going to accept that answer do you Izzy? I think you'd better get a manager for me Izzy right now.'

It was also, somewhat difficult to give a customer that undivided attention when a manager was standing an inch from my ear screaming, 'Come on guys, let's get those calls down, 72 calls waiting'.

As for keeping customers waiting, sometimes when a customer was on hold and became tired of waiting they'd simply hang up; this allowed a brand new caller to automatically come through on the same line. As the line was on hold the call handler knew nothing about the change of customers until they came back only to find a bewildered and angry new caller on the line. This caused some very interesting conversations.

There were various databases, live internet based programs and customer records, all of which had to be opened and ready to use from the start of the shift. There was never a seamless transaction from one to the other and the more programs open on the computer, the slower each one ran.

It took at least fifteen minutes to log into the PC, phone and everything else before a shift even started so we had to arrive early.

While I was still having issues with my headset, I was also trying to get to grips with the *hold* and *mute* buttons. This caused many "Hello" conversations.

'Hello, welcome to ....'
'Hello.'
'Hello.'
'Hello... can you hear me?'
'Hello.'
'Hello – is anyone there?'
'Yes. Hello.'

'Oh for the love of...'   click...

This was the point when I realised the mouthpiece was still poised above my head or the hold button was activated so the customer couldn't hear a word.

Headsets were extremely sensitive and could apparently even pick up the sound of a gnat farting in China, so putting a finger over the end in an attempt for the customer not to hear, didn't work. The customer always heard if a naughty word slipped out or their parentage was doubted out loud. The *mute* button was my saviour for such conversations.

Red and green LED lights flashed various call statistics and figures at us throughout the day: apparently someone, somewhere, at some time thought this hideous piece of technology would nicely offset the neutral wall of the centre.

In reality it served no purpose whatsoever other than to upset more senior members of the workforce. The higher up the corporate level a person climbed the edgier they became when the numbers on the board rose. Anyone at the bottom of the company ladder could virtually ignore it.

The wretched thing was linked directly to the telephones and indicated the number of calls waiting to be answered and how long the next caller in the queue had been waiting. It also showed the number of calls that had been taken that day and the percentage of calls that had been abandoned by customers who'd lost the will to live before they even got through.

The callboard had a direct bearing on how stressed the managers got and how likely we were to get yelled at for overstaying 24 seconds on our break or sipping our coffee flavoured hot water too slowly.

Staff on the front line usually ignored it because it was impossible to speak to more than one customer at a time anyway. It didn't help us to know when there were 184 calls in the queue or that the longest had been holding for 37 minutes; this simply meant the next caller wouldn't be happy and would want to tell us all about it because naturally, this would be entirely the call handler's fault.

Perhaps forewarned is forearmed: either way, we had to take the flack, make the apologies and deal with each call because everybody else was either already on the phone or hiding in the toilets.

There was nothing like a lively call board to wind managers into coiled springs. "There are ONE HUNDRED AND EIGHTY SIX calls waiting!" they shouted, vainly attempting to yell loud enough for staff, but not the customers to hear, even though we all knew those headsets picked up everything.

If the customer also worked in a call centre she was sometimes able to empathise, although it was more likely for the customer to hear the manager squawking and ask what the hell was going on. We were left to explain as best we could.

Each customer deserved 100% of our attention and the calls waiting were not our problem so I tried never to even glance at the flashing fiend on the wall.

When calls became too bad and customers too abusive, I could always rely on *Big Red* to get me out of a sticky situation. *Big Red* was the aptly named 'terminate call' button and although physically it was the same size as all the other keys on the phone it was my savior on quite a few occasions. Its misuse was also one of the fastest exit routes from the call centre.

I once had a customer on a full-blown rant: swearing, hurling abuse and calling my entire ancestry, sexuality and humanity into question. *Big Red* stopped her dead in her tracks. One click and she was gone.

If I ever reached the point where I had to either press it or snap and go on a wild, snarling, swearing rampage through the office, then I pressed it. All abuse, aggression and nastiness just stopped; immediately and extremely satisfyingly…

If only ending all bad calls had been that simple. Anyone caught using *Big Red* without good reason got a severe warning and further misuse meant they were awarded the DCM (Don't Come Monday) award and swiftly escorted from the premises. As with everything else, each time it was pressed, it was logged and fed back to the team leaders.

Sometimes the customer simply forgot to hang up so there was no other option than to cut the call, although it was often highly entertaining to hear the customer saying how useless/pointless/f***ing c**p they thought we were or how they had no idea what the devil we'd been talking about.

Any customer part way through their tirade of foul mouthed abuse when the verbal axe was lowered, often called back to complain. Their original call could be traced from their telephone number and was pulled and listened to by the managers.

Some colleagues, sneakily snared by the system, pointed out that in their highly distressed state, having been on the receiving end of extreme verbal abuse, they may just have accidentally knocked Big Red. This happened quite a few times to me…

One customer I will admit to hanging up on had called back after speaking to another colleague who'd had difficulty in finding the make and model of car the man had just purchased. Noting the colleague he originally spoke to was a newbie, I told the man I'd try to find the details myself and opened our database.

'Ok Sir, please confirm the make and model'

'It's an Aston Martin.'

'Ah, I see, I believe my colleague thought you said *Austin* which would be a classic car. I'm afraid we don't currently insure Aston Martins. I'm really sorry but you'll need to call a different insurer.'

'Oh for Godsakes; let me speak to a man...' he was clearly not impressed with my explanation.

Without any hesitation I hit Big Red with an enormous amount of satisfaction and secure in the knowledge my manager would back me on that occasion. She did.

The *Mute* and *Hold* buttons were also very helpful. *Hold* was used to entertain the customer by blasting them with a shudderingly awful and distorted vaguely recognizable excuse for music while we got a manager or transferred the call to another department.

The *mute* button allowed us to silence the customer while we voiced our opinions on their intelligence to anyone in the office who cared to listen or communicated our tea or coffee preference to a colleague on their way to the machine. The caller waffled away oblivious.

However, if we forgot to check the mute button was working when sharing such opinions on a customer, things became very interesting, very fast.

The other useful button was the *not-ready* button; it was used after a call to give us time to type up notes or just compose ourselves and meant no new calls could come through until we were ready for them. The time spent in not ready was also monitored to the second and if we dawdled too long without very good reason we were in trouble.

Being caught in *not ready* having a chat with a colleague was a major mistake.

4. Call Centre Politics

One thing I learned early on was to be nice to everyone from day one, otherwise a career could be ruined before it had even started. On my first day in the inbound call centre, I was shown into a room near reception with sixteen other newbies who all appeared to be younger than myself. There was a welcome drink on the table and a few snacks for us to nibble on.

After a while, an incredibly bubbly chap in a suit and tie caught my eye. I'd seen him chatting to others and clearly now it was my turn. Gushing with enthusiasm and with a megawatt smile he strolled over and held out his hand. 'How are you?' he beamed, grabbing my hand and shaking it firmly, 'What do you think so far? Tell me a bit about yourself.'

I figured he'd probably never worked in a call centre before, because cynical old me thought his cheerful demeanor would surely have been thoroughly squashed out of him within a few weeks. Perhaps first-day nerves were playing a part.

Wierdo! I looked around the room and was grateful to see the personnel manager heading in our direction.

'Just letting you know we'll be going into the meeting room for the welcome speech in about five minutes so please make your way through the door.'

'Yup, sure, give me a few minutes.' Wow, suit-man was confident. He turned back to me 'It's all been completely overhauled and I think it looks lovely don't you?'

'Yeah, it's OK.' I couldn't disguise the

indifference in my voice. Worrying I may have sounded a bit rude I added, 'It's got great views hasn't it?'

'It sure has.' Suit man was doing the eye-contact thing now and with a mahoosive brilliant white toothy smile he added 'I'm sorry, I didn't catch your name...'

Bored, and with a mouth full of salmon and cheese canape, I said 'I'm Izzy... and you are...?'

'Ah,' he said, holding out his hand to offer another gripping handshake, 'I'm Horatio Hutchinson, Managing Director. Welcome to my company.'

I learned the call centre lingo very quickly. It was a tool for survival in those shark-infested waters.

The first skill was sign language. Occasionally when having a difficult and complex conversation with a customer, a manager would appear, point at himself, then at his desk; clearly he wanted to say something. I'd give a thumbs-up then spend the rest of the call worrying what I'd done this time.

If my mate Jo walked past on her way to the coffee machine: she'd gesture drinking coffee then gagging, (nasty vending machine) or pouring while smiling, (going to the kettle - better coffee). Or she'd sign 'T' with her fingers. Would I like a cup of tea? Simple, yes?

There were other more complex signs. Wide eyes and a pointed stare at someone combined with a look of horror, meant, *the manager you are moaning about is standing right behind you.* Index and little fingers extended together pointing at head and other finger slid across the throat meant, *stop checking your mobile-phone the boss is coming.*

Pulling a clown face and pointing at your head while circling your wrist meant, *this customer is a Muppet.* A sock puppet hand gesture meant *this customer has verbal diarrhea.* The 'shaking-the-bottle', gesture meant *this customer is winding me up something chronic.*

The extended middle finger with or without the accompanying index finger, meant; Y*ou jammy bugger, aren't you lucky to be going home now while I have four hours, thirty-seven minutes left of this utter hell?*

Waving your arms above your head while staring at your manager and pointing at your ears meant you wanted your manager to listen in to the call.

Standing at the desk and gesticulating wildly could mean someone on the phone was giving a bomb scare so do something fast, though the same gesture could also mean *get me some fags if you're going out,* so it was clearly important not to get them mixed up.

Sometimes total concentration was necessary on a call, perhaps for a quietly spoken caller or someone who didn't speak English too well or maybe just a bad connection. Invariably, however, this was also when a manager would attempt to impart some vital words of wisdom using hand gestures and lip movements. While it was perfectly acceptable to shoo away anyone else interrupting with the universal *please go away* gesture, this was easily confused with the two fingered street interpretation of the very same sign so caution was vital.

Most centres had seating in pods; rows of four or five

desks facing each other with a desk divider in the middle, so it was only possible to see the tops of colleague's heads.

Communication by lip-reading and eye contact was only possible if one person stood up. The divider was used to pin photographs on, together with inspirational phrases from the company in their attempt to encourage us to work even harder.

This building also had all the windows screwed firmly shut; the lower floors possibly to prevent undesirables getting in and the upper floors again probably to stop staff from leaping out.

The official reason for window locking was so that the air conditioning could work properly, though having said that, in most of the places I worked, the air-con was either full on or broken. Nobody ever knew what to wear because one day it was ice cold and the next day, when everyone was dressed in thermals, it was off and everyone slowly roasted. A few days later, when everybody was again dressed in their summer finest, the air-con would be fixed and we'd all turn blue.

Rules dictated that regular staff weren't allowed to touch the air-con settings because so much uneducated fiddling was costly to repair. Apparently the only way to get it adjusted was to email security, who had access to the controls. The air-con e-mail was unlikely to be picked up or acted upon for days, by which time the temperature had already been adjusted and as a result would be put off course again.

There were often micro-climates on a floor; on one side was winter and the other summer, with half the staff having the vapours while others wore winter coats.

Walls were often painted a neutral colour such as magnolia, white or grey, although, in an attempt to jolly some of them up, a single wall could be painted a bright purple, lime green or cat-sick yellow. This wall could affect the mood of those staff unlucky enough to have a desk overlooking it. Oddly, staff who sat opposite the purple wall had an uncontrollable urge to eat chocolate all day.

In each call centre the staff themselves were always a wonderful mixture of colourful characters. I was drawn to the eternally happy ones who were liked by everybody, could chat for queen and country and were always ready to help. Some were so consistent in their positive attitude I began to suspect they were smoking something other than tobacco during their regular forays to the car park for a 'quick smoke'.

There were the glamorous ones, those never to be caught, even at 7am, without full make-up, complete with eyelashes and lippy. Conversely, there was always a grungy, tattooed, pierced, baggy-clothed one who looked as if they'd spent the night on the tiles followed by a kip on the park bench on the way to work.

Every office had the ambitious few, clambering up the career ladder as fast as possible; progress meant they no longer had to take incoming calls; although once they reached a team leader position, they had to take over any escalations from their team members.

There was always a loud person whose voice could be heard several pods away, they provided amusement to the rest of the staff, especially when their one-sided conversations were overheard, causing knowing glances between co-workers.

Often there was a quiet or shy worker who arrived early, worked hard and left without speaking to anyone other than customers.

There were always those staff who took the mickey by calling in sick or with 'childcare issues'. They somehow managed to get away with it despite everyone knowing they were sitting on a beach somewhere tropical, having been dim enough to put photos of it on social media.

I felt sorry for first-time mums just back from maternity leave. Often all they had to talk about was the new baby and its bowel habits. Their whole life having changed forever by their little bundle of joy, then returning to work only to find they no longer had anything in common with the other youngsters in the office whose eyes glazed over with boredom as soon as the baby was mentioned.

The office gossip was one to keep in with as was the immaculately turned-out flamboyant chap who was everybody's friend and knew all the juicy gossip about everyone.

Students were usually only working to make money to get them through until their studies ended. These were always the funniest because they didn't give a hoot about the job and didn't put up with any abuse from customers. Most of them were still young and naive enough to want to retaliate if they got any verbal abuse.

Students tended to get away with a lot because they'd happily do hours upon hours of overtime at very short notice for very little pay and so the company let them keep their heads. I admired their bulletproof ambition.

Finally there were those who didn't want the job in the first place but had been told by the Job Centre that they had to get a job or their benefits would be stopped. They turned up late and were already outside before their shift officially ended. They were rude to the customers and would happily tell them massive porkies just to get the customer off the phone.

Most of the latter types were on a mission to get sacked so they could go back to claiming Job Seekers Allowance, an ambition in which they were devastatingly successful.

Many centres had an informal dress code which meant office wear was unnecessary and staff could wear whatever they liked within reason. It was interesting to see the vastly different interpretations of '*within reason*'. Apparently staff felt more comfortable and relaxed in their own clothes and if the customers were on the other end of the phone what did it matter what the staff were wearing?

There were usually a few basic rules to be followed. Jeans were OK unless they were ripped, T-shirts were good unless they had logos which may have caused offence and skirts had to be worn with tights if they were above the knee. Long shorts were OK but not short shorts. No flip-flops and no visible bits of inappropriate flesh which may have distracted other colleagues.

These rules were always pushed to the limits. One young, tanned, very slim girl came to work on a hot summer day wearing a neon pink extremely skimpy top; nobody said a word in objection.

The following day a considerably older and much larger lady wore an identical top, albeit in a larger size, but she was bursting out of it just about everywhere possible. She was told to go and change or cover up which she argued was unfair. The matter escalated until the union got involved. She was rightly very upset about it.

A word of warning; working in a call centre will not improve your waistline. Dieting at a call centre is an exercise in futility. Whatever your weight on your induction day you can guarantee to double it within a few months. Gobbling your bodyweight in chocolates to counteract the boredom and monotony is in the company handbook.

Many companies knew fresh fruit was good for people and healthy staff statistically took fewer days off sick, so they kindly provided fresh fruit for their staff. However there were lots of birthdays and other celebrations which meant plenty of chocolate cake, cupcakes, carrot cake, vanilla cake, fudge cake, tins of Quality Street, Celebrations and Roses, biscuits, pizza and sausage rolls.

Often sweets were bought as team rewards if a target was hit or if the office had been particularly busy or just perhaps because the bosses believed if they fed the staff enough they'd be too fat to get another job.

Call centre life was often so tedious that the only way to alleviate it was to collaborate with the confectionery machine and eat yourself to death.

We all saw many training films in our first few weeks, there were lots of wild and wonderful subjects to test how long we could stay awake. Some films dated back to the 1980s and featured flares, kipper ties, long hippy hair and porn-star moustaches. We were encouraged to take them all seriously.

Over the years I saw so many versions of The Security film, the Money Laundering film, The Fraud film, the Data Protection film, the Fire Awareness film and the not to be missed Health and Safety at Work film that I could have conducted the training myself.

The Workstation film demonstrated how to adjust the chair, monitor and keyboard to avoid any back problems, wrist problems and eye strain. The chair had to be adjusted to a level where staff could sit with a straight back with their feet flat on the floor.

Office chairs could be moved up or down, swiveled, tilted back or forward and the back lowered or raised. When staff were first taken to their new desks they dutifully spent ages fiddling with the chair adjustments until all was absolutely perfect, having had it hammered home by the film how important it was to get everything just right.

Just a day or so later their chair would probably have been altered by someone who had borrowed it because their own broke; that is if, there was still a chair at all...

If it had gone altogether, the only option was to go and pinch somebody else's chair and deny all knowledge when the email came round plaintively appealing '*Has anybody seen my chair? It was set especially for me as I have a bad back and I need it for medical purposes. It has '**Jon's chair**' written on it in tip-ex*'.

It wouldn't be Jon sending the e-mail though. It would be Erin who'd had 'Jon's chair' since Sylvia left three weeks before; Sylvia having inherited it from Jon when he was sacked the previous Christmas.

Busy call centres often involved 'hot desking', which meant nobody had a permanent desk. This was usually because there were simply not enough desks for everyone. With shift working, part-timers, people off on sick, holiday or days off, potentially it meant never sitting at the same desk twice in a row, so no one could personalise their work station with family photos or reminder notes.

Only those colleagues nobody wanted to mess with ever had the same desk on two consecutive days. Although if they ever had a day off, all bets were off and their chair, monitor and workstation would have been changed to suit their stand-in. Nobody ever put a workstation back as they found it: family photos on the desk divider were missing or facing the wall and often there were coffee cup rings, dirty cups and sticky stuff adorning the desktop. This was accepted as normal and was just one more thing to be dealt with before 9am.

Most UK call centres had a security guard on the front desk, for some reason often named Dave, Mike or Steve. It was wise to become acquainted because the security guy knew everyone and enjoyed a chat and a bit of office gossip to relieve the boredom.

More often than not the security guy knew more than the managers about office politics, hearsay, gossip and suchlike.

Security was always priority and Dave, Mike or Steve always took their job very seriously. Everyone had to wear their pass at all times and either run it through a security gate or have it on show on a company embroidered lanyard to gain entry to the building. In one workplace we had to swipe ourselves out as well as in, so big brother knew where everyone was at all times.

The security pass stated the name of the company, the wearer's name, staff number and photo and had to be worn on a lanyard around the neck like the noose of death. The dreadful things always made my neck itch and regularly dunked themselves into my coffee. Lanyards were great to fiddle with as a stress reliever when on a bad call although all the stress fiddling made the clips loose and so they were frequently lost or dropped down the toilet.

Staff who lost their pass had to have their manager come to reception to sign them in.

It was the rules that everyone hated their pass photo; it was usually taken without warning at some random moment during training week, often after a team bonding game so everyone looked shifty and sweaty with their hair in a mess; there was no time to get gorgeous. Many of the mug shots wouldn't have looked out of place on a police "wanted" poster. As a rebellious, albeit feeble, act of revenge most staff wore their pass facing inwards.

To make sure everything was running smoothly staff were each given a regular one to one meeting with their manager. Individual performance feedback was given and any issues discussed, followed by a general chat.

Since it was guaranteed time off the phones, these meetings were eagerly anticipated. Sadly they were often cancelled at the last minute if the centre was busy, the boss was busy or simply forgot.

Preparation for a one to one was vital as this

was often the only chance a staff member had to shine and prove what a fabulous asset they were to the company. Proof of individual statistics needed to be shown with evidence of any work completed above and beyond the call of duty. This was the time to work out any issues and convince the boss of his team member's fantastic personality traits and 100% dedication.

The first one to one was usually held about three months into the job. Up until this point a team manager probably knew nothing about an individual as a person. He didn't know their background, jobs history, achievements, or whether they had any psychological mad axe-murderer tendencies.

As the centres were generally busy with many calls waiting, the managers often never found out about their staff. Figures and performance were always discussed but anything else became unimportant when there were calls waiting because calls were always priority. I never felt my one to ones were completed properly or even that my manager ever even read through my notes. This proved to be a good thing because I used to take the same notes and set of statistics to every one to one I ever went to and nobody ever noticed.

Although lots of preparation was required for the 121, there was rarely any time allocated off the phones to do it. We were meant to gather figures, feedback and charts to support our work in between calls, although it was impossible to write worthy and meaningful notes when calls were virtually back to back with customers demanding 100% attention while they spewed obscenities at us.

Time after time I'd start preparing the one to one notes in all good faith only to have to drop everything the minute I heard the BLEEP in my ear. There was no time between calls to even pick my own nose let alone write notes. Just as I thought of the perfect prose for my one to one there was that damn BLEEP and my train of thought left the station without me.

Another aspect of the call centre life which was commonplace was the return to work interview. After each period of absence each member of staff was taken aside by their manager and given a set of questions to answer giving their reasons for being off. It was often the same set of questions for every absence.

Q1)   Why were you absent from work?
A1)   My Granny died.

Q2)   Did you visit your GP about this?
A2)   There didn't seem much point to be honest.

Q3)   What can we as your employer do to help?
A3)   Can we offer reincarnation?

Q4)   How likely is this to happen again?
A4)   Pretty unlikely, I'd say.

It was widely believed that employees who socialised together outside work, worked better together in work and so there were frequent attempts to arrange off-duty social events. However, since each team consisted of people of different ages and social and ethnic backgrounds, activities like paint-balling or a night out clubbing didn't appeal to everyone.

Together with childcare issues and different shifts meant a team bonding event was a logistical nightmare and therefore rarely happened.

The team did attempt to arrange go-karting once, however at least half the team dropped out citing 'family commitments' a week before and three more dropped out with a day to go with apparent sickness. On the day only three turned up and one of them was an hour late.

To lighten the monotony, staff also organized themed charity days where everyone paid the princely sum of £1 to look ridiculous, all in the name of having fun. There were onesie days, pyjama days, transvestite days, wear something pink/green/red days, various saints' days, Halloween and back to school days. The most enthusiastically anticipated theme day was Christmas jumper day, where competition was fierce to wear the most hideous over the top flashing and singing knitted excuse for a jumper while trying not to sweat to death.

On occasions like Red Nose Day or Children in Need, which were TV led charity events, we all went completely over the top raising money. Often staff all donated to get the Managing Director to spend a day on the phones. Only the bravest MD would be up for such a challenge, if only to prove what a stellar example they could set. Often, after an hour, two at a stretch, on the front line, they'd suddenly remember an important meeting or simply disappear, to the whispered jeers of 'lightweight' and 'chicken'.

I have hilarious memories of the MD in one call centre taking a nasty complaint call while dressed as a chicken. The customer refused to believe any manager would answer the phone in person and convinced she was being lied to, demanded to speak to his superior. As he had no superior, and as usual this was unnecessary anyway, he passed the call to a team leader about six levels his junior because she was the only one available. She dealt with the call with ease.

5. Customers Tell Porkies

I'd been in the sales department of the motor insurance company for a few months and the monotony of having the same conversations over and over with customers became yawningly tedious. I also began to notice things which didn't quite ring true.

Some customers rang for insurance quotes but became edgy, evasive or told whopping porkies when asked specific questions. This meant further questions needed to be asked.

'Do you have any driving convictions?'

'Why do you need to know that?' (Translation, 'Yes I have but I don't want to tell you because it may cost me more on my insurance').

Customers frequently denied any driving convictions though admitted to points on their licence. It had to be explained, often in simple terms, that points on a driving licence meant they had a driving conviction.

It was blindingly obvious when the customer was trying to hide something;

'Have you had any previous claims?'

'Ah, well, er um, no, I guess not.'

'Have you made any claims on your insurance at all in the last three years?'

'Well this idiot stopped in front of me at a green light...'

'So, did you claim on your insurance?'

'Well the whole of the front of my car was all smashed in...'

'So you made a claim on your insurance?'

'Listen sunshine, I can't drive a bloody smashed up car can I? Anyway, it wasn't my fault.'

'So did the other driver claim against you?'

'He better bloody not've done. It was his own stupid fault.'

'Has your current insurer reduced your no claims bonus?'

'Well I don't know do I?''

I had to keep asking the same question in different ways because customers firmly believed if they drove into the back of a stationary vehicle, it wasn't their fault.

Others would say their car was stolen which they said wasn't their fault; agreed, usually it wasn't someone's fault if their car was stolen; unless they'd been stupid enough to leave it parked with the keys inside, which happened, a lot. However, if they had made a claim and their insurer had paid out, their no claims bonus was reduced, which is why the no claims bonus is called a no claims bonus and not a no blame bonus.

It wasn't only the customer who told lies. Sometimes it was the staff who were encouraged to bend the truth a little; often this was exactly the right thing to do.

If a customer had spoken previously to a member of staff who'd been helpful, they often asked to speak to the same person again the next time they rang. This was largely unnecessary because everybody was trained to the same level and should have been able to help. Transferring a call was usually a huge deal.

To transfer a call, the customer had to wait while the call handler found out firstly who the previous staff member was as often the customer couldn't remember. Then which office, city and even country they were in, whether they still worked for the company and whether they were available. Finally whether they wanted to or were even able to speak with the customer.

It often involved far more time trying to locate someone than it would have done to deal with the call in person in the first place.

As a general rule the person answering the call was in a far better position to deal with a call than anyone else and so call handlers were encouraged to inform the caller the other person was unavailable. As every second spent with the customer on hold counted against the call taker, it made sense even if the other member of staff was free and sitting at the next desk.

If the customer really did need to speak to someone else, it was easier to email the member of staff to call the customer back although naturally, this being the real world, sometimes the customer refused to hang up until they were put through.

Customers regularly tried to pull a fast one and said the last person they spoke to had told them various far-fetched and blatantly unbelievable things. We often knew they were lying because on checking the customer's notes it turned out they had spoken to the same member of staff on the first call.

Customers were often confused about no claims bonus. In brief, a customer's bonus was reduced by two years for each fault or unsettled claim made by or against them. The only way it could be retained was if it had been either protected or settled in full, with all losses recovered from the other driver's insurer.

To give an accurate quote we needed the accurate amount of no claims bonus. If the customer didn't know this, the only way to move forward was to guess the fault status of any previous claims by asking the customer questions. Once we started asking these questions, the customer often became guarded and bent the truth.

A customer told me: 'Of course it wasn't my fault, the car skidded on a bend and I lost control. It rolled three times and ended in a ditch. How could that possibly be my fault? Are you saying I did it deliberately?'

All the questions a person was asked when they rang for an insurance quote were for the insurers to assess the 'risk' of that person and charge them the appropriate premium. If someone had made lots of previous claims then statistically it was likely they'd carry on making more. The questions were loaded based on risk statistics gained over many customers over previous years.

There were other factors too: If an inexperienced young driver was added to a policy, the premium often drastically increased. Customers often attempted to pull a fast one saying the car was theirs and their teenage son or daughter was to be a named driver using the car only occasionally. If this was true then fine but often it was quite clear they were telling porkies, which was known as *fronting* and was and still is illegal. We learned how to ask the right questions to weed these out: some of the lies we heard were hilarious.

At the end of the call we gave a price for the policy and asked what their most competitive quote was so far. This was asked, not so we could up the price if the competitor was more expensive, but so we knew how to pitch the call. We had to check both policies were like for like, the excess and whether extras were included. It was at that point we found out whether the last ten minutes had been totally wasted or whether we'd get the sale.

Sometimes they tried it on: "What! My last insurer's quote was *half* that - can't you lower it?"

If their other quote was that good why were they calling?

One man was indignant, "But my brother is paying a fraction of that for his car insurance!"

Did his brother have the same car? He didn't. Was his car the same age? No. Did it have the same size engine? No. Did he have the same postal code? No. Had his brother made any claims or had any convictions? He didn't know. How much no claims discount did his brother have? He didn't know that either.

I tried to explain all these factors plus many more would have been considered when calculating both premiums, clearly not listening to a word I said, he interrupted, "but he's my *twin* brother!" as if that made all the difference.

One man rang for a quote but as I began asking the usual questions he screamed, "Listen sunshine, I just want a bloody quote, you don't need to know my bloody address or age or anything else other than my car which is a BMW. Just give me the damn price."

"Sir, I can't give you a price until I've asked all our questions which are all computer generated and..."

"You don't need to know anything else," he yelled, going off on one. "This is bloody ridiculous, you're clearly just a monkey; let me speak at least to the angle-grinder." I *know* he probably meant *organ grinder* but, that's not what he said.

"Sir," I said, trying to stifle a guffaw, "You won't be able to get a quote from anyone without giving your full details."

"I told you I want to speak to someone in charge." he yelled, getting himself even more worked up.

I put him on hold and asked my team leader to have a word. He was clearly bored that day and was happy to speak to him.

The man wasn't happy with my team leader either. He repeated himself and then wanted to speak to the floor manager. After ten minutes of arguing he was told he'd be called back.

He got increasingly obnoxious on each subsequent call and ended up speaking to the centre manager who'd heard the recordings of the previous calls and had enough.

"I just want a bloody price, I've got no time for your stupid questions. I just want a damn price! NOW GIVE ME A PRICE!" the man roared.

"Twelve million pounds, Sir," the manager told him.

"What! That's preposterous, don't be so ridiculous." He clearly wasn't impressed.

"Well then Sir, if you would like a lower price, then you'll have to answer our questions; otherwise you have your price which is what you have asked for. Take it or leave it."

The man hung up and never called back.

Some customers thought it ludicrous that the price we quoted was more than their car was worth. "If it gets stolen," they'd say, "I simply wouldn't bother claiming."

This wasn't the point: a customer could start up his ten year old heap of rust worth £150 and then run over a whole bus shelter full of people or de-rail a train, he, and so many others like him never considered who'd have to pay all the personal injury claims for everyone else involved in such an incident. It was never all about their car.

One lady rang for a quote for her new car: I asked for the details.

'It's a blue Ford Escort,' she told me, proudly. 'His name's Hector'.

'Thank you. Is Hector an estate?'

'No he bloody isn't.' she was quite annoyed, 'He's actually in very good condition. How dare you!'

Another customer called sounding slightly the worse for alcohol. 'I am not happy at alllll,' he slurred. 'You've given me a car inshuranch policy ending in triple shix.'

I wasn't quite sure what he was getting at. 'Is that a problem?' I asked.

'Is that a problem? Is that a bloody problem? Offf course itsss a bloody problem. Would you take a car insshurance policy with a triple shixx in it?'

'Er, Sir, it's just a policy number…'

'Well, young lady, I don't want your polissssy number. Would you want a car inshhurance policy number with shix shix shix in it?' His belch nearly deafened me.

'Um, it's not anything I've thought about really.'

'I want a different number, a diff-er-ent one, d'you hear?'

I couldn't tell whether he was serious or just

drunk. 'Sir we can't just change a policy number. If you want us to cancel one and take out another then we can but you would incur cancellation fees.' As anticipated he went off on a drunken splurge of abuse, but thankfully appeared to drop the phone and cut himself off in the process. I have no idea if he ever called back or if he even remembered calling us at all.

A further common type of call was one where the customer was just a bit too eager to take out the insurance. Often right at the start of the call they'd ask how much notice they needed to give to take out a policy. Generally people could take out a policy to start anything up to 28 days in advance or they could call and start the policy immediately if, for example they had just bought a car and wanted to drive it home.

The warning flags always went up if someone rang and asked if we could start the policy an hour ago or a few days ago. Usually they'd either just been stopped by the police for no insurance or had been in some kind of accident and genuinely believed we would be able to cover them after the event. This would be back dating cover and was (and still is) illegal.

After few months of these kinds of conversations, I needed a new challenge and needed to keep my brain active so I moved from sales to the customer services department.

6. How Not to Impress

After I'd moved department, I was still at the same staff grade so I was forever looking for ways to get noticed, hoping it may lead to promotion.

In an attempt to improve my time-keeping, I decided to buy a motorbike to cut my journey time from an hour to twenty minutes. An added benefit was I could also park it in the company car park.

I bought a Kawasaki EN500 in black and chrome, a low rider with big handlebars. Colleagues lurking in the smoking shelter often did a double take when I rode into the car park because as I'm quite small the bike looked bigger than it was. I'd passed my motorcycle test years earlier and due to the low centre of gravity on the bike, despite its size, the handling was light.

In the interest of safety and to look the part, I wore full motorcycle leathers; although my interpretation of the biker-chick look was perhaps a bit extreme. The trousers were laced all the way down each leg, the boots each had six silver buckles and the jacket had long tassels; all topped off with a bright pink helmet.

One morning I was caught in a heavy downpour on the way to work and was soaked to the skin. I was so late and so eager to get out of the soggy, heavy, stiff leathers that I decided to get changed in the lift.

My office was on the tenth floor and the lift was usually extremely slow. I already had my getting changed routine down to a fine art and could complete it in one minute flat; I wore leggings under my leather trousers and a long top rolled up under my jacket. So off with my boots, whip off my leather trousers, roll down my top and I was good to go.

On this occasion as I yanked at my trousers in my haste, the wet leather got stuck around my ankles. Hopping on one foot and leaning on the wall of the lift, I stepped on one trouser leg and tried to lift up the other to get them off... it was no good: they simply wouldn't budge. As I leaned against the wall and yanked at my left leg, the lift shuddered and I was caught off balance. I uttered a few extremely unladylike phrases very loudly, just as the lift stopped on the third floor. As the chime sounded to announce arrival of the lift, I realised I was leaning on the doors and only just managed to avoid falling out of the lift onto Horatio and five other suit-type VIP's who were waiting to get in. They were all staring at me with an expression of bemused bewilderment. I hurriedly gathered my scattered belongings from the lift floor and mumbled something incomprehensible. My face was burning beetroot as I attempted a smile.

'Good Morning,' Horatio smiled at me as he and the others politely stepped over my soggy stuff and huddled in one corner well away from me.

'I, er, got a bit wet.' I said sheepishly as if that explained my chaotic state of undress in front of the MD and his VIP guests. I finally made a hasty exit, gathering my soggy leather trousers, still dangling from my left leg and grabbing my helmet, jacket and bag from the lift floor.

'Izabelle...' called Horatio from the lift. Was my agony ever going to end? '...your boots.' He was holding up my soggy boots by the very edges arm outstretched as if to put as much distance as possible between them and himself.

Devastated that the floor hadn't opened up and swallowed me, I reached my desk ten minutes late, flustered, sweaty and still damp. The rain had soaked through everything and I knew I'd have to sit in damp underwear all day.

The minute I got settled, my manager came over to remind me that the MD was showing some extremely important visitors from overseas around the office. He stressed all desks were to be tidy and we had to be on our best behaviour as it was vital the guests were left with a good impression of us all.

If my performance was their first experience of British women, I apologise profusely for letting the side down. I finally got my act together and logged into my phone. To my great relief there were no calls waiting and I slowly regained my composure. As I did so I heard my colleague whisper loudly, 'They're here.' I turned to see Horatio and the VIP guests enter the floor. They were being given an introductory talk by the floor manager. All colleague chit chat stopped and everyone pretended to be busy.

After their talk the VIPs began to tour the floor. Desperate and eager to make up for my earlier display of bungling ineptitude I decided to demonstrate my true professionalism. There were no calls waiting so I picked my moment and just as they came into earshot I said loudly and clearly and in my best extreme smiley voice, to my non-existent customer, 'Good Morning, welcome to InsureYourself.com, Izzy speaking. How may I help you today?' Surely that would impress them and Horatio would realise I wasn't a complete blithering idiot after all. It clearly worked because they stopped, turned to me and smiled. I returned a warm and cheery wave with eye contact. ***Hell I was good!***

'Ah,' said my floor manager to the VIP's, 'Here's a call now if you'd like to listen in. I'm sure Izzy wouldn't mind.' With that he plugged in a spare headset and offered it to them to listen in…

I could only do one thing; I looked reproachfully at the floor manager and said, 'You've cut them off!' I can only hope I never get found out.

I felt a tiny bit better when I discovered that my friend on the complaints department had actually shooed the VIPs away when they approached her with a tin of chocolates because she'd been totally immersed in a customer complaint and hadn't realised who they were.

A few weeks later, I was locking the bike in the car park when Horatio Hutchinson appeared, his megawatt smile aglow. 'Good Morning Izabelle, what a lovely morning for a bike ride.'

I was flattered he'd remembered my name although in my case that probably wasn't a good thing. What had I done this time?

'I wondered,' he went on, 'if you'd be able to offer me some advice? I was thinking of buying myself a small motorcycle to travel to work and thought maybe you could advise me which type I should go for?'

I was stunned. Horatio Hutchinson, Managing Director, was here in the car park asking *me* for advice! This could be my chance to shine. I told him the best places to look and we had a long conversation about bikes, engine sizes and restrictions.

'Thank you so much,' he said, 'I won't keep you from getting to work; I can see you're in a hurry.

Have a wonderful day.'

It was rare for a for a Managing Director of a company to even acknowledge the existence of we ordinary serfs and minions but this MD was different

A while later I arrived at work to see a little step-through moped in the car park. The tiny thing made my bike look enormous when I parked alongside it. I wondered who owned it. While I waited for the lift, Horatio came out of his office. *Oh shit - am I late again*? I wondered.

'Good Morning Izabelle,' he beamed.

Possibly not: at least he was in a good mood. I sneaked a look at my watch. I could just make it providing the lift wasn't delayed...

'What do you think of my new machine?'

'Your what? Er... I... Ah! Yes! Oh, that's yours! I see! Well, I think it's, um cute.' *Cute!* What the hell was I saying? Cute implied it was not a serious bike and how patronising was that? I really didn't mean to be, but he was making me nervous just by being there. And as anyone who knows me well will testify, when I'm nervous I invariably say the wrong thing. 'How did you find it in the traffic today?' I was still gobsmacked that he even remembered my name, let alone that he was chatting with me as if I were a real person and not a mere minion!

'It's ideal for the traffic.' he said, 'really nippy, you know. It saved so much time getting to work today.' He flashed me his beaming smile.

I was aware that I was running late again and my team leader was sure to have something to say. Pulling the *MD just wanted a chat with me* line was wearing thin. The lift arrived so I rushed inside, babbling, 'Oh, lift's here! We'll have to have a race round the car park some time soon!' I joked. Damn, I thought, now he'll *KNOW* I'm a total idiot.

The following Monday, running late yet again, I left home and a mile or so down the road saw Horatio on his little moped chugging along at a leisurely pace.

My bike isn't built to go at a leisurely pace. If I overtook, would he think I was showing off? I so wanted to make a good impression but I had ten times the engine power and if I didn't pass him, I was going to be late again. I had no choice, I pulled out to overtake, in my haste missing a gear and as a result revving the engine like a total novice. I got my act together and sailed off, hoping he hadn't noticed.

Without any further noteworthy incidents I continued working in customer services where my role was to ensure existing customers were dealt with professionally and correctly when they wanted to change something on their policy mid-term or when they had any general queries or complaints.

It was here, that the great myth of customer service was completely obliterated. 'The customer is always right!' What a steaming pile of tripe. Ninety five percent of the time they were confused, misinformed, trying to pull a fast one or just plain wrong.

Lead a customer to believe he was right and a call could only ever go in one direction; south. Equally, if the customer ever sensed fear from the call handler they'd go straight in for the kill. We always had to sound totally confident in our answer. The moment we sounded unsure, the customer went for the jugular like a hungry vampire. This was one of the first lessons we learned and we learned it fast!

One day the company introduced a right little gem of a course called *Thank you for complaining*. What on earth were they thinking? As if the customers didn't complain enough, without encouraging their appalling behaviour by thanking them!

Apparently the idea was to thank the customer for bringing problems to the attention of the company so issues could be addressed, making the company a better one in the future. In reality it was a joke.

Each complaint was dealt with depending on whether it was a real complaint or merely a common whinge.

The definition had to be made because the follow-on processes were different. A whinge could be addressed on the spot and apologised for but then so could some complaints. A customer sometimes said 'I want to make an official complaint.' Aha! A genuine complaint! Then they'd whinge about waiting on the phone for over five minutes. Because they said it was an official complaint it was logged and processed as one although it was actually only a whinge.

Next customer: 'I've had to wait to get through again.' It was the same problem, but this ranked as a whinge rather than a complaint because they didn't say they were making a complaint. I didn't get it and neither did most of my colleagues. Whenever either came through to me, my stomach hit the floor and I did as much groveling as possible in the vain hope they would forget about the complaint and move on. Logging an official complaint took *ages,* there were many forms to fill in and it meant my stats would be shot for the week.

Sometimes the complaints weren't justifiable; for example the customers didn't like it when we charged them extra for missing a payment or for changing their vehicle even though these fees were listed in the contract they had signed. These could be logged and closed because they were standard processes and in the terms and conditions. Some complained about the hold music on the phone line.

Either way it all confused the hell out of me I wished they would just quit whinging altogether and make my life easier.

The customers carried on complaining and so, a few months later and for a change of scenery, I moved to the motor claims department. I thought it would be more interesting and I was right.

There were also complaints in the claims department although about different issues. The most common was about their excess; which was the first £50 or more of a claim payable by the customer directly to the garage and agreed at the start of the policy. In the event of a total loss it would be deducted before the payment was sent. Customers often denied knowing anything about it.

The excess was there as a buffer so insurance companies didn't spend all their time dealing with minor claims. It could sometimes be recovered from the other insurer.

Sometimes the customer had a payout of virtually nothing after all the excesses had been deducted.

I lost count of the number of people who rang

to scream that after a claim they had no car and couldn't understand why they still had to pay the remainder of their insurance premium.

The insurance contract was for the insurer to provide vehicle insurance and the customer to pay the full premium quoted. If the customer chose the option to pay over twelve months, it was merely a credit agreement for their convenience and didn't change the amount due.

If the customer claimed after one week and the insurer paid out, the insurer had fulfilled their part of the contract and the customer still had to fulfil theirs by paying the remainder of the full premium.

Some insurers allowed a change of vehicle following a claim, up until the original renewal date, subject to a premium adjustment to reflect the details of the new car, although it was down to the insurer. The customers who didn't understand spent ages arguing loudly with us.

Many people refused to listen to any explanations from us because they had their own ideas of how things should be. A man whose car was stolen on day ten of his policy told us we were nothing but common thieves who were stealing his money as the remaining annual premium had been deducted from his payout. They paid out £25k for his claim. He'd paid them £27.62. He wasn't happy.

"What the HELL are you doing taking £600 from my cheque? I only had ****ing insurance for ten ****ing days."

'Yes Sir, but we have paid out £25,000 for your car and so you still owe the remainder of the annual premium as well as the excess…'

"Get me your manager…"

These days most conversations with customers are recorded and continually monitored. It's like an aural version of Big Brother. Managers also listen to random calls "for quality and training purposes". Any call can be pulled for dissection and listened to, there is nowhere to hide. Software is now capable of picking up any raised voice or vocal tone and can even be programmed to pick up particular swear words.

One of my calls was picked up and monitored from a time when there was no customer on the line. I'd called the DVLA for details about a vehicle involved in a claim and got the recorded, 'Press 1 for this, 2 for that, 3 for the other and 4 for something else' menu. Then a further, 'press one for this and two for the other' and so it went on, five different menus, terrible music and a frustratingly long wait.

There was no button for 'lost the will to live,' so I held on a while longer while I was led round in circles. Meanwhile my break time came and went. I was put on hold many times and cut off twice. I may also have uttered the odd naughty word or maybe even two to nobody in particular as there was nobody on the line.

I finally got through to a person and noted the full call had taken twenty-seven minutes for a very short answer. It had been an extremely frustrating call.

Four weeks later, I applied for promotion for a job I had already been doing as a stand-in for four months. I wasn't even offered an interview. I asked why as I was better qualified than the person who was offered the job and had been with the company much longer. I was told that my attitude on calls was very poor and needed to be addressed.

I pushed them further and found out they were referring to the DVLA call. A manager who'd never met me had been monitoring my calls that day and had selected that one to judge my entire career on. She decided my attitude was bad on that call alone.

Feeling extremely disheartened by this unfair appraisal of someone who didn't even know me, I decided it was time for another change to forward my career and so I moved to the motor claims department.

7. Motor Claims Department

The claims department was there for when things went wrong, and sometimes things went very wrong indeed.

Part of my role was logging new claims over the phone and making an informed guess at whose fault each claim was likely to be from the description. I also had to establish whether there was any personal injury to either party. Customers never made this part easy.

'Well, you see, the red car came out from the left and then this lady in the mini came from the other side and then the lorry went into the T-junction and hit the blue car.'

'Ok... so, where were you when this happened?'

'In the other road, by the lorry.'

'Which was the main road?'

'Where the Mini was going of course...' Clearly I was the stupid one.

It was best to take as much information as possible and then get the customer to follow up in writing with a drawn diagram. When the drawing arrived everything often became even more confusing because on the description underneath, it said something like 'The blue car hit the white car and then it hit the lorry'. I had no idea if the Ford was the blue car, or which car 'the lady' was in or who went where. It often took a long time to unscramble it all.

The customer would often want to be reassured that an accident wasn't their fault; usually when it most likely was, although at that stage it wasn't for me to say.

'I hit the car but it was parked at a ridiculous angle, so it wasn't my fault was it?'

'But, you hit a parked car!'

'Well, yes, but it was parked at a stupid angle so how was that my fault?'

Fault could only be decided after looking at the facts, diagrams, witness statements, third party statements, police reports and anything else we could obtain. Nothing was ever certain until this had all been done and even then it was often still debatable.

Another old chestnut we heard a lot was 'I swear the other car came from nowhere.'

Tempting though it was to ask whether there were also little green men driving it, I held back.

Some people attempted to submit extremely dodgy sounding claims and it was our role to keep an eye out for anything that just didn't ring true. One claim involved a third party apparently rolling backwards at a set of lights into our insured's car, damaging the front of it quite badly. This in itself was slightly unusual as a car rolling backwards was usually only minor damage if any at all.

We looked at the other driver's statement which said our insured had driven into them from behind. When we read the witness statement we noted the location was a set of traffic lights at the *bottom* of a very steep hill, making it highly unlikely that anyone would roll backwards into the car behind as it would have had to roll *up* a hill. The driver evidently believed it was worth trying to embellish the truth.

Most customers were keen to call us as soon as possible after the event and some were clearly still in shock, a few even called from the accident scene.

One evening I was on the late shift. It was

fairly quiet in the office, we all had our headsets on and were managing to indulge in a bit of friendly banter when my headset *bleep* sounded. Our conversation was killed dead and autopilot kicked in; 'Good evening welcome to Insureyourself.com, Izzy speaking. How may I help you today?'

'Er, 'ello?' came a little cheery sounding voice. I detected a Yorkshire accent.

'Hello Sir. How may I help you today?'

'Er, well duck, it's a bit like this, er I'm in a bit if a predicament you see…' Yorkshire men often use the word 'duck'. I have no idea why. It's pronounced as the word *look* and is a term of endearment, not to be taken as any form of insult. It's like saying *love* or *dear.*

'OK, How can I help, you're through to Izzy in claims.'

'Well duck, my car's been 'it by a lorry.'

'Oh dear, I'm sorry to hear that Sir, are you OK?'

'Well I think so, duck. I can't really tell. If it's OK I'll carry on talking to you.'

'Of course you can talk to me Sir, could I take your name please?'

'Alex Smith, but you sound nice so you can call me Alex.'

'OK Mr Smith, er, Alex; do you have your insurance policy number there please?'

'Er, um, no duck, sorry, as I said I'm in a bit of a predicament…'

Something from the way he was speaking gave me the impression there was a bit more to this call then at first appeared.

He continued, 'You see, as I say, my car was

'it by a lorry and I'm a lorry driver by trade. I was OK you see so I went to see if the lorry driver was OK, because he wasn't moving, I thought he was in shock. Anyway, he was OK but he were worried about his lorry so you see duck, I popped underneath to check his lorry was OK, because I thought his engine may have gone you see and I'm a lorry driver by trade so I know a bit about lorries and…'

I wasn't sure if he was drunk or winding me up or whether he was just one of those people who had to give their whole life story before getting to the point. I needed a few more personal details before I took the incident details so I could find his policy and log it properly so I had to stop his chatter to get it.

'OK Sir, could I take your vehicle registration number please so I can trace your policy?'

'Ah, yes now I can see that from here …' and he gave me the number.

I found the policy. 'OK Sir so you were hit by a lorry; where are you now?'

'Ah, now that's the problem, you see duck, I'm under t'lorry…'

'What, sorry, you're *under* the lorry?'

'Aye duck, when I got under the lorry to check it out for the driver, the lorry was 'it by another driver and now I can't get out because it is jammed against my car. I'm still jammed in here you see, but I don't know where anyone is and I thought as I have my phone I should call you and let you know. I had your number in my phone from before, you see, when my windscreen broke and I hoped you'd be able to 'elp me, so to speak.'

I was rendered momentarily speechless by this last comment, he didn't appear to be the usual type who was calling with nothing better to do on a Friday night than to wind up the staff. He sounded genuine.

''ello, love, are you there? I'm sorry about this but if you wouldn't mind talking to me, I think they've called the emergency services...'

It was possibly the most surreal conversation I've ever had with a customer in all my years of call centre work. He was genuinely trapped under a lorry on the A72. Since I was a qualified first-aider, I knew I should keep him talking. Perhaps it was the shock making him hyper chatty.

We talked about his family and his dog, a springer spaniel called Jess, who had a passion for daffodils. We also discussed the weather, his holiday, his favourite football team and anything else we could think of.

Eventually I heard sirens on the line in the distance becoming louder and louder and finally voices which I took to be the emergency services. Finally he asked my name and said he had to go as they were about to get him out.

By the time I'd finished the call my whole team had gone home. Even my team leader had tired of waiting next to my desk pointing at his watch, so I'd gestured for him to leave. I was alone and the huge office was quiet and eerie.

I eventually left half an hour late, even Dave on security was almost asleep as I passed him in reception.

I tossed and turned about for ages that night wondering about the poor man trapped under the lorry. The next day in work I mentioned it to some team members; none of them were even remotely interested; they each had their own stories to tell and although each call meant a lot to the handler, it meant very little to anyone else. That was the nature of the call centre.

I did have a peek at the claim notes a few weeks later and saw the man had called in since that night and was luckily OK. At the end of the claim he sent me a thank you card which was put on the wall of the office.

Eventually I was promoted from the frontline phones to a claims handler position. This involved being assigned individual claims files to manage in the back office and happily I moved away from inbound calls.

One of my first new cases involved a customer who'd submitted a new claim but had no current insurance with us.

I rang him. 'Hello, I'm calling about the claim you've submitted to us for an accident this morning.'

'That's right, some idiot stopped in front of me at a green light and I ran straight into him; stupid man. When can I get my car fixed?'

'Mr Drew, the policy number you put on your claim form expired six months ago and wasn't renewed. I need your current policy number in order to proceed.'

'Uh? Whatd'ya mean, it wasn't renewed?'

'We sent you a renewal notice asking for payment if you wanted to continue with the insurance. We received no payment.'

'I did pay. The garage sorted it out for me I spoke to you from the garage when I bought the car eighteen months ago. I paid over the phone.'

'Sir, the insurance only lasts a year then you have to renew it. Did you get our renewal letters?

'I never got no bloody letter and I never knew I had to send in another payment!' He was becoming agitated.

I checked his address hadn't changed - it hadn't. I asked if he recalled receiving our renewal notice.

'Well yeah - you sent me lots and lots of junk but I threw it all in the bin. I hate junk mail.'

'Sir, that wasn't junk mail; it was your car insurance policy paperwork. On the outside of the envelope it clearly said there was important information inside and not to discard the letter until you read it.'

'All junk mail says it's important. I'm a busy man; I don't have time to read every damn thing that comes through my door.'

'We sent you the first letter two months before your cover ended, we sent a further reminder a month before to remind you and then a final one once your insurance had ended to warn you that you no longer had any cover.'

'I never got any of your stupid letters only rubbish which I told you I don't have time to read and so they went straight in the bin. I didn't even read them.' He was getting irate and louder now. 'Why didn't you phone me instead of bombarding me with junk?'

'We did call you Sir, but our notes say you told us you weren't interested and you hung up on our adviser.'

Quite simply, he wasn't insured. Finally, just as I thought the message had sunk in, he said, 'So anyway, when can I get my car fixed?'

Mr Michael was a young driver who had submitted a claim which was under investigation as we suspected there was something he wasn't telling us. He called us daily for an update but there was little we could tell him until the assessors had interviewed him. We couldn't tell him the reason for the delay so we had to play for time.

He'd bought a brand new flash sports car which had been his absolute pride and joy and it had cost a fortune. He'd saved up half the money and been given the rest by his parents for his 21st birthday. On his third day on the road, he'd lost control and rolled the car which had landed on its roof in a nearby ditch, writing it off. No other car was involved and nobody was seriously hurt.

The recovery company provided a report to the insurer, as is usual, but it mentioned a few vehicle modifications. The insurer, unaware of any modifications being declared at inception, decided to investigate.

Mr Michael was extremely anxious to get news of how his claim was progressing and each time he rang he became more irate at the lack of progress. Finally the truth emerged, once he'd bought the car, he and a few mates had fitted a 'few little extras'. These turned out to be a full body kit, lowered suspension, new performance exhaust, low profile tyres, an upgraded engine, bucket seats, tinted windows, sports decals and a number of other what he called 'small extras'.

The first problem was that he'd done the work with his mates rather than getting it professionally done. Lowering the car had made the vehicle unstable so when he hit the bend at speed the lowered suspension possibly caused the car to lose control.

The second problem was that he hadn't mentioned any of the changes to the insurer when he first took out the policy only days earlier, preferring to tell us the car was, in his words, 'totally standard'.

The result of this little indiscretion was yet another customer screaming, full volume at me, because the insurer refused to pay his claim and voided his policy. Had he told them about the lowered suspension they wouldn't have covered the car in the first place. The body-kit alone would have attracted a higher premium because it made the car highly attractive to thieves and so increased the theft risk.

After he'd finished screaming he said quietly, 'My mum's going to ferkin kill me'.

Some phrases were said so often by customers that the mere mention of one sent the hairs on the back of my neck into overdrive. Invariably it meant the customer hadn't understood anything I'd just spent the whole call explaining to them or thought they'd get a different answer by being as arsey as possible.
"It's just not good enough,"
"That's ridiculous!"
"Get me a manager!"
"'I want to complain!"
"That's absolute rubbish!"
And that old chestnut, "You listen to ME, I'm your customer!" often followed by the urban myth, "Weren't you ever taught that the customer is always right?" What a steaming pile of tripe that one is.

Those phrases were spat at me by customers so often I heard them in my nightmares. They caused much eye-rolling amongst the staff who knew the words meant a long arduous call would follow.

The very worst types of customer knew the opening hours and called deliberately just before closing time. These were known as the Midnight Screamers. The poor staff member answering the phone suffered not only abuse from the customer but also enforced unpaid overtime.

When a customer was all fired up, we had to let them vent which always took time. The process meant they wanted to tell us everything over and over until they ran out of steam. In their confused little minds, some truly believed they were getting their revenge by shrieking at a faceless voice on the end of the phone. I doubt any of them would have been as abusive face to face.

After they had vented and calmed down, we were supposed to leap in and fix their issue. It was a self-defeating circle though because the longer they spent screaming at us, the less likely we were to be able to escalate the call to a manager because there were rarely any senior staff who stayed late.

The Midnight Screamer's problems were usually minor but had been blown out of all proportion by the caller's late night ruminations. The hapless operator could almost feel them rubbing their hands with glee, knowing they were keeping us from going home. They were always determined to tell us all their problems, niggles and complaints from start to finish, and any attempt to pre-empt the caller would be met with a loud, 'LET ME FINISH!' The rant would then recommence, from the beginning while the handler watched the other staff log off on the dot, pack up, and with a cheery wave depart for home like a whippet on ice.

As most complaints required liaising with many other departments it was virtually impossible to sort out any issue late at night. Being alone in the office was a little eerie. Perhaps it was haunted by the ghosts of long-dead operatives, pinned to their headphones by ranting callers. I hated being alone there late at night with only Dave, Mike or Steve on the main desk, ten floors down for comfort.

There was one legendary late call which was taken by a colleague I shall call 'Sam'.

A man called late on a Friday night, he was abusive, drunk and hell-bent on causing as much distress as possible to whoever had the misfortune to answer his call. He demanded a manager, he demanded compensation, he demanded a refund and he demanded to be listened to and not interrupted.

It was late in December and the whole team was getting all geared up for the company Christmas party that evening: the early shift staff were already in a local bar, getting merrier by the hour.

The phones had been quiet and the remaining staff had managed to get themselves looking gorgeous for a night on the town in between calls. Hair and make-up was done, party clothes were on and everyone was raring to go. Christmas music was being played on somebody's phone and a few people had bottles of Coke on their desks which suspiciously appeared to be refilling themselves. Perhaps the large empty bottle of vodka under one of the desks had something to do with it. We were all in the party mood. Four minutes until close and counting down...

Sam's face said it all. He threw his hands in the air in mock despair followed by a 'shaking the bottle' gesture to the rest of the team; it was two minutes before 10pm. We all groaned in sympathy as the lines shut to new callers but as an existing call this one now had to be dealt with properly.

Poor Sam stayed at his post, the last man on a sinking Christmas ship. Torn between going to the party, already two hours in, to join the others and showing some Christmas spirit, the rest of the team hovered by the door.

22:15: Sam hadn't managed to get a word in.

22:20: The rest of the team's Christmas spirit was ebbing and a few had left for the party. Those remaining were suspiciously tiddly. The customer kept going at full pelt.

22:30, Sam had enough. 'Right! Mr Ridley, I understand... Mr Ridley... Let me finish... MR RIDLEY... We're getting nowhere, OK, I understand you're not happy, it's now 10:30 at night and my shift finished half an hour ago. I have listened to you for the past thirty minutes and I've heard what you've said... Mr Ridley, we have to move forward...'

In training we were told, when being confronted with a verbal tirade, the best way to stop the customer was by using their name over and over. The tactic was failing.

The customer paused for breath but then clearly took up where he'd left off.

Sam had heard enough. 'Mr Ridley, Sir! Right, ENOUGH! Sir, let's just take a summary shall we? Firstly, I have your name, your policy number and all the details of your complaint together with your phone number to call you back. Now, please confirm you have a note of my name...? You don't? Well F**K YOU then.' With a wicked grin he hit Big Red, stood up and looked at us. 'What the hell are we all waiting for? Let's go have a Merry Christmas!'

I had my own way to deal with the *Midnight Screamer*:

'Hello, hello… dear me, sorry no, the office is shut, you'll have to call back, I'm sorry, they've all gone. Who me? No, sorry I'm just the cleaner my lovely, sorry, bye.'

Or, using my best monotone voice, 'Hello, I'm afraid the office is currently closed. Please call back between 8am and 10pm Monday to Friday. Thank you for your call, it is important to us. Goodbye.'

8. The Loss Adjuster

After a few years with the motor insurance company, I moved to a loss adjusting company where my job was to take new calls from the public following household incidents such as fire, flood or burglary. I had to check their insurance cover then deal with the whole claim until completion. Although I worked for and was paid by the loss adjuster, as far as the customer was concerned I worked for the insurer. This was intended to avoid confusion.

I took my first few calls with the trainer sitting next to me. 'Good morning welcome to Insureyourself.com, Izzy speak...' My trainer was horrified; I'd reverted to autopilot once the headset was on and answered the phone with the previous company's name. The customer launched into her call, clearly not noticing my gaffe. I was sure I could often have answered a call and told them I was the Queen of England and they wouldn't have noticed. I doubted they ever listened to the greeting anyway.

Sometimes the claim was so new, I'd be speaking to the customer while the Fire Brigade was still on scene: it was my job to locate alternative accommodation for the customer when required, find someone to temporarily board up the property, inform the drying-out and post-fire cleaning company and guide the customer through the many steps involved to get back into their home.

I had to make sure any fire damaged electrical items and furniture were replaced along with everything else, work out costs and ensure the whole process went as smoothly as possible. Some customers needed virtual hand-holding throughout and called almost hourly whereas others were happy to call us every few days.

There were the odd few who shouted at us because they didn't understand the limits of their policy or why certain things weren't covered.

We each had our own caseload which meant a lot of our time was spent off the phones. However, it was a call centre as well: and frequently, just as I was getting stuck into a large and complex file, a new call would come through which had to take priority. As I was dealing with many different claims at the same time, by the time I'd finished the new call, I'd often forgotten the details of the original file and have to go through it all again.

Naturally, by the time I got back to the first, yet another call would come in. It would have been nice to be able to do one thing at a time; still at least it wasn't all phones.

To keep us motivated we kept a notice board to display photos which the customers sent us to support their claims and illustrating their various misfortunes. In the middle we put our *Snap of the week*. One week there was a photo of a one day old, Lamborghini: all freshly polished and gleaming in the sunshine outside a huge country mansion, its owner standing beside it, grinning broadly.

The second photo featured the same car only hours later. The front of the car was still immaculate but the back end was a black skeletal mess.

After a brief maiden voyage, the owner had returned home, put the car back in the garage and gone into his house. A short time later, his house fire alarms had gone off and the cause was the car in the garage which was well alight. He managed to get the car out of the garage while it was still ablaze without too much damage to him or the house. It appeared a lit cigarette end had been sucked through the air intake while the car had been out on its maiden voyage and this had set the car alight with catastrophic results.

I loved the loss adjusting job; it was not only interesting but I found it especially satisfying weeding out any dodgy claims and flagging them for the fraud team. These types of claims cost insurance companies billions each year, causing an increase in everyone's premiums.

Some suspicious claims stood out like a shark in a fish tank…

A man rang to report a new claim where he said his fish tank had leaked causing a bit of damage. The fact it had been referred by the insurer meant there was something they weren't happy with. I began with the basics; what had caused the leak and what was the damage?

'Why are you asking so many questions? I told you my fish tank leaked and damaged some stuff.' He was rather too vague.

'Where did it leak and what did it damage? Do you know what caused it to leak?' I was only asking logical questions but he had clearly not anticipated any interrogation. 'Look, it just leaked OK and it's damaged my computer. Are you calling me a liar?'

That was a red flag. I'd merely asked for more information and he was already going off on one.

'Of course not, Sir; however I need the full details to register the claim here on our systems…'

'Why can't you just send me a form like they usually do?' Clearly this wasn't his first claim.

'I'll be as quick as I can; so do you know what caused the leak?'

'Er, well I think the fish did it.'

'The fish…'

He sighed loudly. 'Well, um, I think the fish pushed an ornament over in the tank…'

'OK…' something was clearly fishy about this one. I bit my lip and noted the time of the call to ensure it could be pulled at a later date, 'and then what happened?'

'It made the tank drip onto my new computer and it's damaged that as well.'

At this point I firmly believed he was embellishing the truth. He knew I knew. I knew he knew I knew.

'So, the tank has dripped onto your computer which is also damaged, was anything else damaged?'

'I dunno.'

'When did this happen?'

'Er, a few days ago, why the hell are you asking me all these stupid questions? I don't have time for all this crap.'

'Just a few more questions Sir then you can go. You'll need to keep the tank and the computer in case we need to see it. '

'What? Are you ****ing serious? The ****ing thing was broken! Why the hell would I keep it? Are you calling me a liar?'

'No, Sir, of course not; it's standard practice to ask you to keep damaged items so that we can inspect them if necessary. Do you still have the computer and fish tank?'

'So you are calling me a liar! This is ****ing ridiculous! Of course I didn't keep them. Why on earth would I keep bits of broken glass and an old computer?'

'Can you tell me what type of computer it was?'

'Er... A brand new Apple laptop.' He proceeded to give me the full spec and model number.

'Do you have the laptop as we can get it assessed for you?'

'Oh, for **** sake, why would I keep an old broken laptop? Of course I don't have it, I threw it away with the bloody fish tank. I haven't got time for all these stupid questions. I'll call you back.'

I waited for him to hang up first and as he did so heard him say to someone in the background, "Sh*t. they want to see the f***ing laptop."

As I attached a post-it note to his file with the word FRAUD on it, I considered my own fish at home. I had kept fish for years and they'd never knocked anything over. Even if his were very big fish big enough to knock over an ornament hard enough to cause damage, wouldn't that have caused a crack and a huge whoosh of water rather than a small, slow drip? The pressure in a fish tank can be enormous.

Not many people would be daft enough to keep their new laptop underneath a fish tank either.

The customer appeared confused as to whether it was an old computer or a new computer but of course I couldn't call him a liar...

The file was dispatched straight to fraud.

Mrs Fisher was a sweet, 82 year old lady who'd had a chip-pan fire.

She'd tried to throw the flaming pan outside her back door and had dropped it, sustaining third degree burns to her hip, legs and feet and losing all her hair in the process. She'd only just come out of hospital following the incident and had called us on the advice of her neighbour.

The unfortunate lady couldn't apologise enough. 'I am so very sorry,' she said, 'It was my own silly fault not keeping my eye on the pan, you see the phone went and I… you don't want to hear that anyway. I really didn't want to call you at all: it was my fault. I'm such an old fool. Mrs Stapleton next door says I can claim a new one, because you see, the old pan was damaged.'

I looked at her policy and she had the full cover for buildings and contents. I asked what else was damaged but she told me it was only the chip pan she wanted to claim for because she needed it to cook as she couldn't stand for long on her poor burned legs. I pushed further and she admitted the kitchen was a bit of a blackened mess as well.

It appeared the whole kitchen was severely smoke damaged, floor ceiling and units. The back door had melted and the house smelt terrible. I was almost in tears by the end of the call. I wanted to get round there and help her myself but she lived the other end of the country. She was adamant she didn't want to claim for a new one because, she said, it was her own fault.

I managed to persuade her to let our loss adjuster go to visit her. She only agreed if I was able to send a female as she was nervous of all male callers. Our adjuster went to see her that day and made sure she claimed everything she was entitled to and not a penny less.

I thought about all the lying, cheating and scamming people I'd spoken to over the previous months and this poor old lady was ashamed of herself and didn't want to be any trouble to anyone.

I'd been with the loss adjusters a few years and was actually enjoying it: when out of the blue I had a call from a brand new ski company which was just setting up in the area. They were to specialise in taking groups of twenty or more enthusiasts skiing to America. They needed someone passionate about skiing, with experience in customer services.

The job wasn't in a call centre and I was told I would be visiting American ski resorts regularly either alone or escorting large groups of skiers, sourcing new hotels abroad and in between trips, working in the office in the UK. If I could have written my own perfect job description that was it.

The directors had met me on a group ski trip I'd been on which they'd organised the previous year. They told me I'd impressed them so much with my enthusiasm for skiing that I was their first choice for the role. I accepted their offer because I knew I'd regret it forever if I didn't. I wished my loss adjuster colleagues the best and left two weeks later with lots of 'Jammy Bugger' comments on my leaving card.

Just weeks after I'd joined them, I was called into the office and told the business was no longer viable and they had to let me go. I couldn't go back to the loss adjusters, partly because I didn't want to lose face, but also because following my departure they lost the business of one of the major insurers and had make thirty people redundant. There was no job for me to go back to.

Unemployed for the first time ever, I applied for four jobs in the same week and, remarkably, was offered all four. I had one day to decide whether I wanted to start at the bottom as an office junior with an estate agent on minimum wage; work in an inbound call centre for a credit card company; sit at a checkout in a supermarket or work in the motor underwriting department of another large insurance company.

I started two weeks later at the insurance company. At last I had an office job with minimal telephone work! My new job only involved calling customers when I needed to speak to them about a case I was working on.

I called one customer simply for confirmation of his car registration number so we could issue his insurance certificate. It should have taken minutes, without it we couldn't insure him and his policy would be cancelled.

We'd already written to him four times with no response and this was the final attempt to get this one simple answer from him. I politely introduced myself and explained I was calling from his insurance company.

'Not interested!' he said firmly.

'Mr. Harries, I'm not trying to sell you anything: you're already insured with us. This is about your current car insurance and I just need your registration number, that's all.'

'Listen love, what part of *not interested* don't you get? Simple English; I AM NOT INTERESTED. Get it? Do you want me to hang up on you? I'm too busy for this.'

'Sir, we just need this short answer or your car

insurance *will be cancelled* in three days.'

'HELLO? I'M NOT INTERESTED!' He hung up.

So as we'd warned him in the three letters we'd sent him, I had no option but to cancel his policy, which meant he was then driving illegally. A further letter was sent confirming the cancellation. Perhaps he read it: who knows? There was nothing else I could have done. Doubtless when he realised he rang some poor call centre worker and screamed at them. I was only relieved it wasn't me and duly made sure the notes were fully up to date.

Data protection was vitally important: before discussing anything with a customer we had to ensure we were speaking to the right person. There were set questions to ask to confirm this was the case. Only once these were answered correctly we were able to continue.

I rang Mrs Smith, a very deep voice answered, 'Hello'.

'Ah, Hello, I need to speak to Mrs Smith please.'

'Yes, speaking,' said the voice.

'Er, is that *Mrs* Smith.'

'Yes; speaking,' came the somewhat curt reply.

'Mrs Jessica Smith,' I said.

'This *is* Jessica Smith,' replied the gruffest voice I ever heard.

Security procedures also required us to confirm the post-code. The letters A,C,V,P and T, all sounded similar over the phone, as did S and F, so I used the phonetic alphabet; Alpha, Bravo, Charlie... However not everybody knew it. When a customer was on a bad line, with a noisy background and I couldn't hear a word, I checked;

'S.T – is that Sierra Tango?'

'Eh?'

'You said 'S.T. Is that S for Sierra and T for Tango?'

'Uh, I dunno what you're on about, can you speak up?'

'Your postcode, is that S.T or F,P?'

'SP, FP, FT'. Yes.'

'S as in Sierra?'

'S, F, you know S, as in… as in socks.'

'Was that S, socks or F, fox?'

'Yes.'

'Okay… and the last part; was that N for November or M for Mike?'

'M,N,M… like M for mice.'

Sigh 'Was that M for mice or N for nice?'

'Jeez, are you stupid?'

It was far easier to regress to infant school and use the 'A for apple, B for balloon' alphabet, training had made it clear we had to match our language to whoever was on the phone and unfortunately "A for apple" often made more sense!

After four happy years working in the back office, the company opened a call centre on the floor above and talk began of training us to take the inbound calls when it became busy.

On the few occasions I had reason to visit the call centre floor I saw the haunting torment on the faces of the poor souls incarcerated there, like cows plugged in to their milking stations. It was only a matter of time before I too would be told to join them and the clock was always ticking.

A year later the insurer was taken over by a much larger company which already owned several other smaller motor insurance companies.

After the takeover, we could access all the previous notes from any of the companies, this enabled us to offer customers a much smoother transition when they were switching insurers.

Although we could do a lot to help the customers by transferring their no claims bonus automatically, some customers were difficult to communicate with or refused to be helped; for this reason we sometimes found ourselves doing unnecessary work simply to please the customer. This often took far longer but was easier than explaining and taking their abuse.

When the time came to work on the call centre floor during busy periods I didn't mind too much because it was a change of routine and it didn't happen very often. As we never knew which company the next customer would be calling from we had to be very careful to answer with the correct company name.

A "BEEP" in the headphone followed by the name of the company the customer was calling from was the only information we had before the customer was live in our ear. It was vital we heard that information.

'BEEP Company X', or 'BEEP Company Y'.

I then had to give the greeting 'Thank you for calling Company X/Y. How can I help you?'

In one day I could potentially take calls for

fifteen different companies. If I missed the company name I had to muddle through and work it out from the policy number. The customer always sounded suspicious if I asked them which company they were calling and it was hardly professional.

Apart from a few underwriting differences, the processing of the policies was all identical, all done using the same system on the same computer with the same software.

It was also important to send letters with the correct headed paper. A man called to ask for his no claims discount to be sent to him immediately. He complained that his new company had requested it twice and they were threatening to cancel his policy if he didn't send it. I explained, as I had done for so many customers before him, that his Renewal Notice *was* his no claims bonus and had already been sent three weeks earlier.

He didn't understand. 'Don't give me that bull****,' he said. 'Just send it to me and I never want to hear from you again. Your company is total **** and I'll never ever use you again.'

I asked him to confirm whether he'd received his renewal documents from us.

'Yes I did and your price was astronomical so I threw them in the bin. You're taking the piss if you think...'

'Sir, you just told me you had your renewal letter. That renewal letter *was* your no claims bonus, so you *have* had it and you threw it away. Not to worry though, I can sort it with your new company now for you.'

While he'd been spewing forth obscenities at company X, I'd done a sneaky search of his details and discovered his car was now insured with company Y, both sister companies, owned by the same main company, both underwritten in the same office by the same staff.

I could have transferred the bonus from one to another in under a minute.

He wasn't happy. 'What? What! That's ridiculous! Are you refusing to send my no claims to me? I want a manager, it's my right. Are you going to send it to me or shall I speak to your manager? Really this company... I will NEVER deal with you again ever...'

'But Sir I could help if...'

He was having none of it. 'I'm telling you I never got my No Claims Bonus and I want you to send it NOW. You have no right to withhold it. The way your company has treated me is appalling and I'm disgusted with your attitude. Total bunch of cowboys, complete tossers... I expect to receive it in the post tomorrow or there will be trouble.'

I spent five minutes re-issuing his company X No Claims Bonus letter for him, printing it on the correct headed paper, getting it franked and taken to the post room where it was posted it out to him. Two weeks later it arrived back on my desk with a covering letter addressed to Company Y saying how relieved he was to be rid of Company X who he said were total idiots and who had finally sent his No Claims Discount after a considerable amount of messing him about.

I updated it exactly the same as I would have done two weeks previously over the phone only now it was four weeks late and by then Company Y was a day off cancelling his insurance.

9. High Volume Complaints

After eleven years the whole office was closed due to the recession so I needed a new job fast. By this time I had young children and needed part time hours to fit around my family. With mounting horror I realised the only places offering the hours I needed were call centres.

I managed to get a job in a high volume call centre for an online grocery delivery retailer taking calls from members of the public who had issues with their shopping deliveries.

Whereas previously I had worked in call centres where customers called when they wanted something, this time customers called because they were angry and wanted someone to shout at. The good side was the calls were mainly short; the downside was they were almost all complaints and there were *a lot* of them.

If I had thought call centres were awful based on previous experiences, I had a whole new experience awaiting me. This one was hell itself.

With no idea of what was to come, the first day was quite lighthearted and began with some recordings of real calls to give us a flavour of what was to come. I should have run for the hills then. The first call recording was probably just to break the ice and it made all twelve of the new recruits howl with laughter.

'Hello. I am calling to complain, I have just got a pizza out of the freezer for my kids' tea and there's no topping on it whatsoever. Nothing at all, I'm appalled, it's a bloody rip-off. What the hell am I to feed the kids?'

'I'm so sorry to hear that Sir, I can certainly give you a refund and…'

'I don't want a bloody refund I want a bloody pizza that is why I bought the damn pizza; to feed my kids. This is ridiculous. What are you going to do about it?'

'Sir, could you tell me which pizza it is please so I can log it.'

I don't bloody know because THERE'S NO BLOODY TOPPING aren't you listening to me?'

'Sir, I mean the make, the brand as we will have to inform the manufacturer.'

'Jeez… I'll get the box… It's your own make pepperoni, deep pan, seriously, was the guy wrapping it too stupid to notice? There's absolutely *nothing* on it, no cheese, no tomat… Oh.' There was an awkward silence. 'Ah, just a minute, oh shit. Er, oh. There's bloody stuff on the bottom, what the Hell..? Ah, Oh, um,' another silence followed, then, 'Ah! I think I may have been holding it upside down, there's topping on the bottom. Ah sorry OK…' There was a click and then silence. He'd hung up.

Next we were sent to listen in to live calls being taken by existing staff to give us more idea of what our job would entail. For this we had to borrow a headset from the spares box. The size of the new company together with the huge turnover of staff meant I was then re-introduced to the headset as an instrument of torture.

We were told new headsets were on order, but as newbies we would be given a temporary 'older' set until the new ones came. The trainer then appeared with a large dog-eared cardboard box full of a mass of tangled wires and headsets which he dumped on the floor.

Whilst foraging in the box, the trainer reminded us how expensive these hi-tech pieces of equipment were as they were yanked out with all the dexterity of a pig eating spaghetti.

Of course some didn't work; it was a case of trial and error. Most were missing vital parts but all were bent and obviously very well used. Perhaps this should have been a warning sign.

I let the trainer locate a 'decent' one for me. Eventually he yanked a grotty specimen out of the depths of the box and chucked it in my direction. As it landed on my desk, a lump of something gooey and yellow flew out of the mouthpiece and landed on my lap... sensing my unease and as the box supply was exhausted, the trainer then started looking around the nooks and crannies of the office.

He found a set on the floor, wrapped around a desk leg, clearly having been there some time because the faux leather earpiece was cracking with bits peeling off, the speaking part was loose and stuck with a blu-tac and sellotape combo and the cable had been painted in stripes with yellowing Tipp-ex. 'Here you are Iz,,' he said flinging the prehistoric relic at me. When he saw the look of horror on my face, he added, 'it's just for today.'

I found out from my new *buddy* that customers often rang just to let off steam because their apples were bruised, an egg had broken or similarly deeply traumatic events had befallen them.

These weren't customers I was used to who

composed themselves first or waited until the following morning to call; these were angry punters who wanted to vent at someone immediately. It was my ear which took a bashing when their pears only had five days use-by date on them rather than the seven they would have picked themselves.

In the evenings the calls came through thick and fast. Had the driver reversed over their cat or damaged their property, which happened once or twice, I could have understood it but their bananas were too yellow - seriously?

Whatever their problem was, my job was to try to put it right. The calls were usually straightforward but there were so many of them and the vast majority were complaints. It was relentless.

We were shown their version of the headset familiarity film which demonstrated how to wear and adjust it properly. Apparently the headset was our friend although if it was too tight it could cause headaches, too loose and it could fall off and too loud it could cause hearing loss.

The mouthpiece had to sit at exactly the right distance from our mouth so our voice wasn't distorted; any crackles, whistles or excessive changes in volume had to be reported. Hearing loss, they said, was a serious issue and a faulty headset could cause hearing damage. There was a volume button for customers who were too loud.

This, so the film said, was why all staff would receive a brand new headset. It was a full two years before I got a replacement for the manky version I was given on my first day.

The centre was open from 8am until 11pm although

my hours were 3pm until 10pm, when hard-working folk had arrived home after a long day at work and were not at their most friendly.

This company apparently offered a choice of either double or single ear headsets. Double ear sets cut out any outside noise enabling the wearer to hear the customer shouting at them in glorious surround sound. Single ear sets could be dressed to the left or the right and allowed the wearer to hear both the customer shouting and the colleague on the next desk.

The padded earpiece was available in leatherette or sponge. The sponge ones became manky within weeks, accumulating discarded flakes of skin, dried ear-wax, ear mites and other nasties. Looking on the brighter side at least this gave the wearer a few days off work with an ear infection.

The leatherette ones caused sweaty ears but at least a quick clean with an antibac wipe sorted it out.

The new sets were permanently on order which meant waiting behind other staff who'd been waiting even longer and who'd pinch them the minute they arrived.

Once that thing was on my head and I was plugged in, I was part of the national grid, to be force fed calls through that gateway-to-hell contraption until I either walked out or dropped dead.

If it did all become too much, I could forget hanging myself with the wire as there was a break section in the middle; designed so the wearer could move away from the desk without taking it off.

Sometimes the headset ganged up with the telephone to cause confusion and worry to the wearer who would occasionally hear a strange echo on the line. The echo was rumoured to be Big Brother monitoring our calls. I'd automatically get nervous whenever I heard one and consequently said the stupidest things.

Frequently, even worse than an echo, my words were repeated back to me about five seconds after I'd said them, which was highly disconcerting leaving me with no option but to ignore myself. I'm sure everyone hates hearing their own voice on a telephone. Mine sounds like a four year old with gastric flu.

The headset also amplified sounds, especially background noises, which often appeared to be louder than the customer. Sometimes it would be a TV theme tune, or much worse, a screaming toddler where the doting parent had become 'scream-blind'. With the verbal equivalent of Armageddon in my ear the parent would attempt to discuss something important apparently oblivious to anything untoward.

There was no escape from these mind numbingly hideous calls and I had to battle my whole being to stop myself activating the big red button. Occasionally with a silent prayer and my fingers crossed, I'd tactfully suggest that the customer might like to call back later when she was less busy and we could hear each other, in the vain hope she'd perhaps appreciate my distress.

My comments were usually ignored as usually customers wanted a reply right there and then. Quite frankly they couldn't have cared less if their grouchy sprog was deafening me.

In training they mentioned any loud noise through the headset could seriously affect our hearing and we should avoid exposure to it at all costs. Any headset squeals or odd noises were to be reported and investigated and the headset replaced. Health and safety, they said, must come first.

In the actual event though and as we weren't allowed to hang up on customers, we persevered with the call. Though every inch of our being told us to run for the hills, our ears bled and our heads screamed for painkillers; we still had to finish that call.

Once trained, we were straight in at the deep end. During peak times it took a while for callers to get through, then security had to be cleared before we even knew why they were calling, so more often than not they wanted to complain about the wait before they even got to their reason for calling!

Naturally, the longer the complaint about their wait, the longer the remaining people in the queue had to wait, so it created a vicious circle. It often took far longer to deal with their waiting complaint than it took to deal with the reason they'd originally phoned!

Those calls went like this:

Me: 'Good afternoon, thank you for calling, I'm so sorry you've had to wait. You're through to Izzy. How can I help you?'

Customer: 'Hello... Hello, is this a real person? Oh, finally.'

Me: 'I'm so sorry you were kept waiting today. How can I help you?'

Customer: 'Sorry? I've been waiting on this phone fifteen minutes!'

Me: 'I know. I'm so sorry about that; it's been really busy today. How can I help you?'

Customer: 'Do you think fifteen minutes listening

to that bloody dreadful hold music is acceptable?'

Me: 'No, It's awful, I'm really sorry, I know the hold music is terrible.'

Customer: 'It's absolutely dreadful! My cat could produce better music than that.'

Me: (Through gritted teeth but still smiling…) 'I'll make a note of your comments. How can I help you?'

Customer: 'Well young lady, you can help by apologising for giving me a headache, listening to that awful machine music for fifteen minutes.' I always had to take a deep breath at this point: I'd already apologised in almost every sentence: why didn't they just get on with it and stop wasting even more of my time. These calls lengthened the queue behind them and p***ed off even more people I'd have to deal with!

Me: Grabbing the stress ball from my colleagues desk and digging my nails in it hard 'I'm really so, so sorry, we are incredibly busy. Rest assured I'll log it with the manager.'

Customer: 'Log it with the manager? What good will that bloody do? You've wasted fifteen minutes of my precious time! The very least I want is to speak to a manager.'

Me: 'May I ask exactly what it is you want a manager for? I'm sure I can help you.'

Customer: 'I want an apology, young lady, for wasting my time.'

Me: 'OK, I understand you have been waiting and I have apologised, there is very little else we can do when it's busy. I'm so sorry.'

Customer: 'That's not good enough: I'm demanding an apology.'

Me: 'I can get a manager to call you if you'd like

because the only manager here is on another call at the moment. Can I help you with your original query?'

Customer: 'No I'll call back to speak to your manager.'

At this point the line went dead, wasting even more time. Unbelievable!

Besides the callers with kids, there were also very loud TV sets, barking dogs, radios, doorbells, the sound of someone snoring or on the toilet or my very least favourite; someone chewing loudly at full volume an inch from the phone.

Despite being forced to listen to such verbal assaults almost daily, I had to not only understand the caller but also ensure that they'd also heard and understood me. Sometimes even colleagues a few desks away could hear the noisy customers on my phone and me shouting over the din in order to be heard.

When these loud callers came through, with every bone in my body telling me to hang up, the most I was allowed to say was, 'Would you prefer to call back later when you're not so busy?' What I actually wanted to say was, 'your horrendous racket is causing me to become de-stabilised; I can no longer hear myself think and I'd prefer to eat my own ears than listen to this ungodly noise any longer'.

When updating notes on files it was an art to be specific and factual without saying anything which could have been viewed as malicious, defamatory or untrue. The notes went on a file after a call to give an indication of the points discussed on the call. The notes automatically logged the time, date and name of the person taking the call.

We always had to remember that at any time a customer could ask to see these notes under the Data Protection Act and so were encouraged to be purely factual and as brief as possible. So where we would have liked to have written 'Customer was horrendous, absolutely livid and screaming abuse using foul language and threats of violence because her shopping was two minutes late. She appeared to be pissed as a fart. Beware - horrible woman'. Instead we had to put 'Customer not happy - late delivery.'

After two months at the grocery call centre, just as I got used to using their telephones, they brought in a brand new system which had the very latest communication technology. Not only did it record everything, and have the ability to find it again in seconds, the software was capable of logging to the second, how long was spent tying up a call, talking and holding as well as when and how long everyone was on break and when they went home.

It also had voice technology which apparently could spot voices raised in anger and specific naughty words uttered in despair. It flagged up whether the staff member or the customer hung up first, how many calls were less than ten seconds long and it read blood pressure and heartbeat... OK, I lied about the last two, but if it had monitored those then it would have had to introduce an automatic cut-off because of Health and Safety rules.

A weekly list of computer generated statistics was produced for the whole team so everyone could see in glorious technicolour how they compared with each other. The biggie was the Average Handling

Time, AHT, which monitored how effective each individual was by the average length of time they spent on each call. The fewer seconds spent on each call, the more calls could be squeezed into each shift. There were always new ways to shave milliseconds from each call.

So that big brother knew where all staff were at all times, there were phone codes for lunch, break, meetings, training, feedback and referrals, revealing how long was spent by each staff member for each activity. There should have been a code for 'lost the will to live' although that would probably have been overused.

The new telephone system was PC based; a small grid was shown on the screen which detailed the status of the call. Clicking the screen icon allowed new calls to come through.

On start-up day, we all had a nightmare trying to remember what to do and many customers either heard staff asking 'Help - what the ****ing hell do I do with this ***ing phone?' or 'which one do I press for...' and they were cut off.

I couldn't work out how to stop the calls coming through and with no floorwalkers anywhere around I decided my only option was to unplug my phone and go for a walk in the cool night air of the car park before I lost my head completely and started screaming. I wasn't the only one; there were several people standing in the car park that night looking bewildered.

Once the new system was implemented the team leaders watched the call monitor screens like hawks and as soon as a line turned red meaning a staff member had been in the call tie up code for too long, they swooped over to ask if there was a problem; translated that meant, *get back on the phones NOW.*

If a call needed to be listened to, the customer only had to give the time, date and number they'd called from and the call recording could be located and checked. There was nowhere to hide.

Despite being state of the art, the phone system had an irritating quirk. When a customer was put on hold to reach another department, the phone music, evil enough in its monotonous aural assault, was also distorted; it was the musical equivalent of nails down a blackboard.

10. Do You Know Who I Am?

Sometimes callers with complaints used the 'Do you know who I am?' card. I rarely recognised any of their names and the fact they thought they were more important than anyone else made me determined that they would be treated exactly the same as any other customer.

It didn't matter who callers said they were, what they did for a living or who they told me their friends or relatives were. The few genuine celebrities I thought I recognized when I saw their names were quick to ask a question and leave but the ones to use the line in an attempt to gain a voucher, compensation or just to try to intimidate me were usually people who'd once had a neighbor whose sister's friend once worked for the company.

One man told me he was a very close friend of the CEO and could get me fired with one phone call should he so wish. I still couldn't give him what he wanted so he took my name and told me to expect a meeting with my manager about it. Of course nothing ever came of it although I later discovered his CEO *friend*, who hadn't been the CEO, merely a manager, had resigned in a blaze of negative publicity over two years previously for book fiddling.

Jo, a colleague on my team, once spent ages sorting out an issue for a customer. Apparently a mix up with a payment meant her shopping wasn't delivered. Jo spent the best part of an hour phoning different departments, and ruining her call stats for the week. She eventually sorted it and agreed to issue the customer both a refund and a compensatory voucher.

She rang the customer and was careful to explain, many times, that the voucher and refund would take 48 hours to process.

The customer was extremely grateful. 'Thank you so much, Jo, that's absolutely fine. You're absolutely amazing. Heaven is missing the angel that you are. God bless you my love'.

The following day Jo chased the voucher and found it had already been processed so she rang the customer to let her know it would be with her sooner than anticipated.

The customer's reply was unexpected. 'Why on earth are *you* calling me?' she appeared far from happy.

'I just rang to let you know we've already processed your voucher as we discussed yesterday. I wanted you to know it's on its way.'

The customer went off on one. 'You lied to me Jo, YOU let me down, I've spoken to your manager and he's going to have YOU investigated. How dare you lie to me?'

Jo was taken aback, 'I can assure you I said 48 hours, but we've already sent it.'

'No, you're not only incompetent but you're a liar! Your manager has taken this into his own hands and he's going to have your calls listened to and you will be in a lot of trouble for lying to me. Don't *ever* contact me again.'

Jo's calls were listened to and she had given the 48 hour time frame no less than five times during the call. The manager spoke to her an hour later and told her not to worry as the customer was clearly confused.

Some customers didn't even let me say *hello* before launching into their complaint and demanding a manager. I hated those calls: most of the time I could easily have solved their problem had they given me the chance. A typical call went like this;

'Good afternoon, Thank you for calling…'

'Get me your manager, NOW.'

'I need to take a few details first.'

'Are you deaf or stupid? I want a manager.'

'I can't pass you over until I know what it's about and whether I can help.'

With a huge sigh and a huff, the customer gave the details and it was usually something very simple I could have easily dealt with, yet sometimes they still demanded a manager and were extremely rude about it.

'I want to speak to your manager; Now.' It was another one of those calls. 'No actually I want to speak to the Managing Director. No, in fact you know what, let's sort this out once and for all; get me your Chairman.'

'What is the query about so I can try to point you in the right direction?' Had we really done something that terrible?

'This is not the first, not even the second time but it's the THIRD time I have received my shopping delivery without carrier bags.'

'Okaay, so you want to speak to the Chairman of the company because there were no bags with your shopping?' I said it louder than strictly necessary so my colleagues could all have a laugh.'

'Er, yes, that's right.' He appeared to have realized how ridiculous he sounded.

Stunned this was even an issue I confirmed

that as we now had to charge for carrier bags, there was a tick box on the online order form to confirm whether bags were required at 5p a bag and I asked if he had ticked that box.

He hung up.

If I contacted a manager about a customer demanding to speak to them, the first thing they always asked me was, 'What's it about? Who's on the phone and have you done Data Protection?' I was always made to feel stupid if I hadn't managed to get at least this basic information.

Customers seemed to think that by being highly obnoxious from the outset they'd get what they wanted. They were wrong. Sometimes they'd called the wrong department or even the wrong company, so the manager couldn't help them anyway.

One evening an absolutely vile, screeching banshee of a woman demanded a manager because I wouldn't give her a voucher; she was clearly playing the system and there were notes all over her file to say not to issue any more.

Fortunately my manager at the time was incredibly supportive and always stood up for the team, letting us listen in to any calls he took over: it was always satisfying to listen to a customer abusing someone else who had more authority and clout than I did, especially when they repeated my own words verbatim.

Firstly the customer denied any knowledge of her previous 25 vouchers and demanded proof that we had sent them. My manager offered to email the proof to her and asked her email address.

She quietly said 'S for sugar, E for Edward...'

When she'd finished, my manager, being the

subtle type that he wasn't, repeated loudly 'SEXYSLAPPER69@...' and we both hit the floor laughing. I have no idea how he finished the call with a straight face.

Occasionally a customer demanded a manager, just to be awkward. We knew we could help them and not bother a manager, but some customers truly believed they were above talking to a lowly, insignificant regular call handler and some believed they'd get a different answer from a manager.

In order to escalate a call we needed their details.

'Can I just take your details to find your file to pass to my manager? I'll need your full name and postcode please'

'Jones...'

'I need your *full* name please and postcode.'

'Mr Jones.'

'Mr Jones I need your *full* name to find your file.'

'J Jones.'

'What does the 'J' stand for please Mr Jones?'

A big sigh 'John. Now get me your manager.'

'And your postcode Mr Jones?'

'SA24.'

'Mr Jones I need your *full* postcode to locate your file.'

'Oh for godsakes just get me your manager and stop stalling for time. You're a waste of space.'

'SA24 - and the rest of the postcode?'

At times such as these we put the customer on hold and had a word with a colleague on the next desk. The colleague then took over the call and said, 'Hello, I understand you wanted a manager; how may

I help you?'

The customer would then display a major attitude change, as if butter wouldn't melt, and repeat the issue important person to important person. The colleague would then repeat verbatim what the original call-handler could and would have said, had they been given the chance and the customer hung up happily, ego intact.

Sometimes a customer didn't want to bother calling us themselves and got their spouse to call us, but still felt it necessary to scream abuse from the background.

Him: 'Hello, um we've had our cornflakes delivered and the box has leaked cornflakes all over the floor.'

Me: 'I'm sorry to hear that, let me get them refun...;

Her, screaming in the background: 'Tell 'er it's disgusting service an' they're all over the ferking floor'.

Him: 'Er, yes, and there's some on the floor.'

Her, screeching from the background: 'Tell 'er they're everywhere and the effing driver walked them all into the new carpet.'

Me: 'I am really sorry. I'll get them refunded to your card straight away.'

Her: 'Tell 'er, it's a f***ing right mess an' we wants condensation.'

Him: 'Um, Yes love, it's *compen*... sshhh, she's sorting it. It's the wife, yes. Thank you so much, thank you, I'll explain - bye'.

Her: 'Tell 'er it's not good enou...'. Click.

Sometimes customers rang to apologise for their attitude previously saying they had had a bad day at work. One customer even called to apologise for his wife! He said she'd been upset as they'd had a row and thought we hadn't delivered her milk but they had since found it in the fridge. 'Please would you apologise to the lady my wife spoke to earlier in your office, I'm afraid my wife was very rude. I do hope she didn't upset your staff member too much.'

The sad fact was we were all so used to being spoken to in that manner that we had become virtually immune.

Quite regularly, elderly customers called because they had problems ordering on-line, having been told by their adult children that online shopping would be easier for them and that it was very simple to do. So, eager to "get with it", they went and bought a PC or laptop just for this purpose.

I guess the majority of people under fifty in the UK regularly use a PC, and for them it is very simple, but older people who never had computers in school and have absolutely no idea how to use them become very confused and extremely flustered. Some have no concept of using a mouse, clicking, highlighting or even the very basics.

''Ello Love. Fred Rogers ere, now listen my love, I'm trying to do my shopping you see on this interweb thing and I, er, well I wonder if you could 'elp me.'

'OK, I'll see what I can do. Can you tell me first what browser you are using?'

'Er, yes, it's a Dell it says... there's a blue screen and it wants a password. What's my password?'

'Is that the PC password or are you on our

website?'

'Uh?'

'Do you have a password for your PC?'

'Well I don't know love, you tell me! Oh hang on a minute my whole screen has gone black. What's happened?'

'Er, has it gone into sleep mode?'

'Well I don't know. How would I know that?'

'Try pressing any key.'

'Where is the *any key* button?'

At this point I knew I was in for a long night.

Another customer rang very irate and frustrated as he couldn't log into the site to do his online shopping. 'It won't work! It won't let me do my shopping! I need to do my shopping. I thought this online shopping was meant to be easy!'

I explained the issue could be down to the build-up of cookies on his browser. I was about to explain how to fix it when he said; 'I don't have any cookies. I'm diabetic!'

With a huge sigh I waved my mate to go to break without me. My AHT was ruined for weeks after that call.

Sometimes a customer wanted something they were never, ever, going to get. Once, a late night screamer rang having a tantrum because his shopping was three minutes late. Customers were usually given either one or two hour slots and this customer had waited for an hour and called the very minute the hour was up. It took him three minutes to get through.

After I contacted the driver on his mobile I confirmed he was only minutes away.

The man threw in the old, 'It's not good enough' and the 'I want a manager now' chestnuts. I explained there was no manager that time of night and besides, the driver would be there in minutes. The man accused me of lying to him and wanted the home telephone number of the Managing Director.

He continued with the 'I'm not getting off the phone until I speak to a manager,' speech. I told him he'd be waiting all night. Finally I told him I'd have to hang up as I'd done all I could.

He then embarked on a full-blown wobbly. As I was about to hang up, I heard his doorbell ring and the line went dead without a word of apology or explanation. How very rude.

One Friday evening in the run up to Christmas I had a call from a customer saying she was only five minutes late getting home from work due to the Christmas traffic and she had missed her delivery and a card had been left by the driver to say he had been and gone. Drivers were never able to leave shopping without a signature from the customer so they had no choice but to return to the depot with all the shopping. This was a pain for all concerned. The customer didn't get their shopping so rang to shout at us in the call centre, the driver had all the shopping in order of delivery so now had to re-juggle the van for the other customers and someone in the store had to put everything back on the shelves again.

As it was Christmas I rang the driver just to see if it was possible for him to return to the customer at the end of his round. By the time I got hold of him he was on his way to the next village. He pulled over to answer my call.

'I've had a ferking gutsful of this shit from this ferking company. I was making good time, I called at her house and all the lights were off and no answer, while I was ringing some little urchin sods were throwing eggs at the van. It's taken me half an hour to do one missed delivery and I have ten more to do in a one hour slot. I'm ferking pissed off and I've just about had enough.' His voice was getting louder, he was not pleased. 'This is the worst blooming job I've ever had and I have a good mind to jack the whole lot in. In fact, fuck it, I quit.' He hung up.

Ah! I clicked back to the customer who was patiently waiting on the line. 'Um I don't think he'll be able to make it back to you tonight.'

The customer wasn't pleased and neither was the store manager when I rang him to rearrange the delivery; apparently the driver had also called him to quit, left the van where it was and gone to the pub.

Some of the most frustrating customers were those who were not content with a simple answer. They wanted to know *what if;* what if the driver didn't turn up? What if they didn't hear the bell?

Mrs Pickering rang as the driver had been but she said she hadn't heard the bell so he'd left a card and returned to the depot with her delivery.

I rang the driver to see what had happened. 'I went to the house but there was no sign of life, no lights on and no car in the drive. I rang the customer and there was no answer so what else could I do but move on? I can go back at the end of the slot if she likes.'

I agreed with him there was only so much he could do. I explained it to the customer who was adamant she had been in. Either way I told her he could return later.

'What if I don't hear the bell? When will he be here?' she was clearly starting to get angry.

'I can't tell you when but within the next hour.'

'What if he doesn't come back?'

'He will come back, he needs to pass your house to get back to the store.'

'What if he doesn't?'

'He told me he most definitely will and he will call you before he gets there to let you know a more accurate time.'

'That's not good enough, what if I miss his call?'

'Well, with all due respect, if you don't get off the phone you will miss his call as the line will be engaged.'

'I think you are very rude young lady and not at all helpful. I want to speak to your manager.'

'I'm sorry I can't transfer you to a manager, there isn't one available. I have sorted out your issue, I've confirmed the driver will be returning as soon as he can, there's nothing more a manager can do.'

'But what if he doesn't return? What then?'

'Well you can call us again but there should be no need.'

She waffled on for a further fifteen minutes, until she realized I wasn't able to do anything else for her.

Two hours later the colleague on the next desk took a call from the same woman who had missed the driver when he returned. The driver had said he had returned just fifteen minutes or so after I had spoken to him but the customer's line was engaged and again there was no reply at the door. She had missed the call because she'd spent so long on the phone to me. Those sorts of customers were the creators of their own problems.

I also had a few laughs with customers.

'I've had my order delivered but I had ordered those mini bread loaves and they are all flat and squashed, it looks like something heavy was packed on top of them but they're inedible. Also I ordered some frozen haddock fillets but they are all wet and defrosted, the box is so wet it's disintegrated.'

'It sounds like some form of bible story you have going on there with the loaves and the fishes. Unfortunately I've not been trained to do miracles yet but would you be happy with a refund and a voucher?'

We both had a laugh and for a while at least my faith in humanity returned.

11. Off The Record

I soon learned ways of dealing with nasty and abusive customers, the ones who freely flung abuse and insults at me, simultaneously demanding a manager extremely loudly. I used my cooling down technique; this involved putting them on hold and going for a coffee to calm down.

I'd queue at the coffee machine, politely letting my colleagues go first and having a chat with anyone I knew on the way back. Often my nerves were so frayed that I accidentally put sugar in the coffee so I had to go back to the machine again.

By that time I was more relaxed and able to return to the phone with a sincere sounding, 'sorry to keep you waiting there, I was looking for a manager for you but unfortunately there isn't one available right now.'

Then I'd then put them back on hold while they were taking a breath to start again and went to get my least favourite manager.

My team leader at one point, Luke, a very flamboyant, young and ambitious sort, knew everyone and was liked by the whole team. He explained he was there for each of us should we need him, he hated lateness or laziness and was, in his own words, 'a really fun guy'.

Luke's only downside was that he had an aversion to taking escalations.

I'd do everything in my power before I referred and escalated a call and I suspect my team mates felt the same. It was only fair that the manager should take those calls - that was, after all, part of their job. However, the moment Luke got whiff of an escalation coming his way, he disappeared and fast. He had it down to a fine art.

Not all calls to the centre were complaints. There was a variety of calls and some customers were lovely people who I enjoyed chatting with. Many calls were easily sorted by calling the driver to check how long they'd be. Many just wanted a credit for a broken item or to organise a return or substitution. Sometimes they'd made an error with their order.

Mr Rich: 'Why on earth have you sent me five bags of bananas when I ordered five bananas? Do you people have no common sense? Who on earth would want five bags of bloody bananas. Are you all stupid?

Mrs Blake: Why on earth have you only sent me five bananas when I ordered five bags of bananas? I can't feed a daycare until full of thirty kids with five measly bananas. Can't you people read?

Both customers had received exactly what they had ordered.

I once had a call saying a delivery was late so I rang the depot only to be told the driver had been detained at Her Majesty's Pleasure the night before and wouldn't be in work that day or possibly for a lot longer. In those cases the job required tact, diplomacy and a few little white porkies.

One man rang screaming blue murder at me because he'd ordered a delivery to his caravan on holiday, but had arrived two hours late, only to find the driver had been and gone with the shopping, unwilling to leave a whole week's shopping outside an empty caravan in the blazing sun.

'You listen here, my brother is Chris Jones the MP, my other brother is an editor at the Times and I am not cross I'm *furious,* do you hear me? FURIOUS and if you don't get my shopping to me I will make sure this is all over the papers tomorrow. You'd better believe me if you know what's good for you. I have seven kids here who haven't been fed all day and my wife's going crazy. What on earth am I supposed to do? How the hell are we supposed to feed seven hungry kids with NO BLOODY FOOD? This is downright ludicrous.'

I explained the driver had been there on time, was unable to leave the food or contact the customer and had therefore left. I pointed out we'd done nothing wrong and there were no more delivery slots available until the next day. I asked him to stop shouting at me.

'If you want me to bloody stop shouting then I suggest you get me your manager NOW.' He shouted, even louder.

I pointed out it was now 9pm and there was no manager available.

'I KNOW it's late,' he roared 'I have eight starving children here and no means to feed them. I've just driven 150 miles and if you want me to stop shouting at you then I suggest you get your bloody manager out of bed.

I noticed, according to him, his brood had expanded from seven to eight in just a few minutes. No wonder he'd hit psycho mode.

'Are you going to explain to six hungry kids why they won't be fed tonight. That's child abuse, that's what it is you are child abusers.'

I'd heard enough and hit the hold button. There was a point when enough was enough and that was it. I noted he'd now gone down to six kids and wondered just what was going on.

By the time I had fetched a glass of water and cleared my head the man had hung up. Perhaps he ordered a pizza; who knows?

A week later a woman rang to complain that her order was late. She too played the, 'My kids are all sitting round the table waiting for their tea' card. I checked her order for no other reason than I could. She'd ordered whisky, fags, cat food, washing up gloves, washing powder, a bottle of red wine, a packet of biscuits, some chocolate and a 24 pack of beer.

Another screaming woman called at 9pm because she was in the middle of cooking for a dinner party and had just noticed the delivery she had received at 10am that day had not included her stock cubes. I pointed out this was because she had not actually ordered any.

My explanation was not good enough. She rattled on about wanting compensation for the whole cost of her delivery, her shopping and her telephone calls which she estimated cost her £1 a minute.

I pointed out she wouldn't be getting anything as we hadn't done anything wrong, the item was clearly not ordered. I also mentioned the call was free and not £1 a minute. She told me while I had been 'prattling away with my feeble excuses' her phone costs had increased another £2, so I activated Big Red to save her any further costs.

We had many customers trying it on and saying something was missing from their order. When I checked their previous orders, I saw they had pulled exactly the same trick numerous times before.

One lady had done it so often her orders were now checked twice before leaving the depot and the drivers even photographed each order before delivering it. Despite this, she still had the gall to call us again to say items were missing. She was finally banned from using online shopping with the company ever again.

Another customer rang because his delivery was thirty minutes late. I chased the driver who had just repaired a puncture and was able to confirm he'd be there within ten minutes. The customer started screaming that I'd ruined his son's birthday party and wanted me to speak to his ten year old son to apologise.

I often wondered what kind of parent planning a birthday party for a child, would leave the party food to the very last minute. Definitely not one who was likely to win any awards for parenting.

Other customers blamed me for making them late for work. One rang, saying the delivery driver had reversed over his wife's cat. Of course, I apologised profusely and asked after the poor creature. He said he didn't give a stuff about the stupid animal, but it had made him late for work and for that he wanted compensation.

I also spoke to many customers who were clearly eating, this was one of my pet hates. Having a customer churning food round their mouth whilst trying to engage me in conversation, was infuriating.

Occasionally my headset picked up far too much information. One customer was only too obviously in the bathroom, and sounding quite breathless. He sounded somewhat preoccupied at the start of the call and was talking rather jerkily about his delivery being late.

I confirmed the delivery would be within thirty minutes. His breathing suddenly became shallow, there was a grunt, a sigh and a silence followed by the sound of the toilet roll being pulled. He came back on the phone sounding a lot more relaxed. I couldn't resist asking, 'OK Sir, are you satisfied with that?'

He at least had the grace to sound slightly sheepish. 'Yes, very satisfied. Thank you.'

'Is there anything else at all I can help you with?' I asked...

My colleagues and I all jokingly suggested once that every call centre worker should have the right to hang up on one customer each week. It wasn't much to ask; it would help preserve sanity and counteract stress for staff – resulting in a reduction of sick days! Win/win situation!

We also thought that just one swear word uttered per staff member, per week, should have been at least tolerated, if not allowed, providing it was justified. Management sadly, disagreed.

A well-known call centre game, used for motivational purposes was the 'word sneak' game: a word of the day was established and circulated and the call taker had to introduce that word or phrase into the conversation with a customer without them noticing. Examples were 'vomit', 'jam-jar' or 'giraffe'. Some were easier than others.

One colleague was a master at the game. When a customer was on a full rant at him he'd say, 'My giraffe just vomited into a jam-jar.' As the customer was on a rant, they never heard him and if they stopped to ask what he had said he'd reply 'No, no; you first.' The customer would continue where they'd left off and the rest of us had a much needed giggle.

Another call centre wheeze, strictly for rare occasions when the lines were moderately quiet was to dare a colleague to stuff as many citrus chews (i.e. Starburst) as possible into their mouth while keeping the phone line open. The faster they chewed the more they dribbled.

Each team of about ten staff in the centre had its own team leader or manager. Their role was to support the team members, address any issues they had and ensure they worked to the best of their abilities.

The best team leaders were those who managed to strike a balance between being friendly and approachable but also took a step back from the team just a little bit to maintain their respect. They couldn't be best buddies with everyone and needed to take control when necessary.

Taking escalations was a big part of a team leader's job and it was important they dealt with them properly. Some managers lacked the skills to do this effectively. Often all they had to do was repeat verbatim what we on the phones had just said but sometimes, when the calls got nasty, they were expected to take over and do the groveling.

I frequently asked customers, 'So, you'd like my manager to repeat exactly what I've just said to you; is that right?'

Providing the team member had given the correct information in the first place, the manager was there to back them up and not roll over and agree with the customer; doing this made the team member look like an incompetent fool and encouraged the customer to ask for a manager the next time they rang.

A woman rang to complain that a delivery driver had spilled bleach on her carpet. She was very rude right from the start. 'Get me a manager. Your driver came into my house and spilled bleach all over my carpet and has trodden it all over the place.' She spoke as if the driver had done it deliberately.

'Oh I'm really sorry to hear that.' I shifted into autopilot, 'Could I just take your details please?'

'Didn't you hear me? Are you deaf or stupid? - I want a manager: now!'

I was determined to get her details first. She was equally determined to be as stubborn as possible.

'Oh for heaven's sake,' she shrieked, 'why are you being so unhelpful? You're supposed to be customer ser-vic-es.'

'I am trying to help you but I need...'

'Oh this is ridiculous, just get me a manager.'

'Your postcode and full name please.'

'Mrs Smith!' she said with a huge, impatient huff. It was clearly another one of *those* customers.

'Thank you Mrs Smith - and your first name and your postcode please?'

'Oh for heaven's sake! This is ridiculous, you're very rude. What's your name?'

I sighed.

'Your name; I want your name. You're very rude, very unprofessional and I've asked for your name, which you're refusing to give to me, and I've asked to speak to your manager which you are also refusing me. I *will* be reporting you.'

'My name is Izzy. Can I take your first name and postcode please?'

'Do you want my bloody shoe size as well? No, I refuse to speak to you any more, just get your manager.'

At this point I just wanted to press the lovely red button on my phone... But I knew the call was being recorded and they'd know if I hung up.

Hanging up was a sackable offence unless a customer used offensive and abusive language; at that point we were told to give one warning and then terminate the call. I regularly willed them to swear just so I could cut them off.

Unfortunately for me, Mrs Smith hadn't sworn or been abusive, she was merely being obnoxious.

I used my cooling technique and put her on hold while I got a coffee, swore a lot on the way there, breathed deeply and walked slowly. If I was lucky the she would have hung up or be bending someone else's ear before I got back.

Unfortunately she was still there. 'Hello there, I am awfully sorry, the manager is busy on another call at the moment, however he's asked me to take your details first and he'll call you back.'

She finally gave her details and I checked her notes. This kind of customer was exactly the type who tried to pull a fast one. My background as a claims handler made me suspicious and finally I got some job satisfaction; I was right.

Mrs. Smith had six other accounts with us and had claimed for something spilled on a table and something on her leather jacket and now she was trying for a new carpet. In fact, due to spurious claims and dubious circumstances our drivers refused to enter her home at all.

I rang the driver who confirmed he'd left all the groceries on her doorstep and hadn't set foot in the house. She'd signed the delivery note.

My manager called her back and explained it would be necessary to send somebody out to her 'to make sure this didn't happen again'.

Predictably, her attitude changed fast. 'I'll call you back; there's someone at the door,' she said and hung up, never to be heard from again. Result! Kudos to that manager for doing the right thing!

Mrs Grant was a cat lover. Every week she ordered 12 tins of cat food; different flavours but always the same brand. She rang us one day to say we'd delivered the wrong flavour and her poor babies would starve because they didn't like tuna. She asked politely what could be done about it.

Occasionally a store would be out of one flavour or brand and so an alternative was selected and offered as a substitute. I checked, and sure enough there had been a substitute of tuna delivered because the pilchard was out of stock. She had signed to say she was aware of this. I asked if she could keep the tins until her next delivery and we could swap them.

Her attitude changed dramatically.

'I don't want 12 tins of cat food hanging around my house and cluttering up the place.'

I offered her an alternative; to return them to the store for a refund.

'I'm not driving down there using my petrol for your error'.

I asked if perhaps the driver could return the next day to swap the tuna for pilchard but she swore she'd be out all day. I asked her what she wanted me to do as all the options I suggested were shot down in flames.

While we were chatting I checked her account. The same scenario had played out a few weeks earlier, when she had ordered tuna but received chicken, previous to that was a chicken/pilchard combo and a few weeks before that it was the wrong scented candles.

The driver always pointed out any substitutions to a customer and the customer was given the option to return the items if they preferred. When I checked this lady's account I could see the last three occasions it had happened, she'd been given a voucher as compensation - this had been noted and the driver had since been asked to obtain a signature to say the customer was happy with any substitutions.

This customer had signed the form but clearly she was pushing her luck for another voucher. The system notes clearly said not to give her any more.

I pointed out she had signed the form.

'I want your manager,' she said, predictably.

I explained the scenario to the manager and mentioned I believed Mrs Grant was trying to pull a fast one. My manager was busy but said to tell her no more vouchers as she'd signed the substitution form.

I went back to the phone and relayed this to the customer. She morphed into a screamer. 'I want your manager now! I will *not* be spoken to like this. You are calling me a liar and I refuse to be spoken to in this way. Get me your manager NOW.'

My manager at the time was not in and a team colleague was acting team leader for the day. He was a wannabe manager and had only been asked to step up because nobody else wanted to do it. He had already acquired the look of self-importance and had spent the whole shift checking everyone was on a call and peeking at all our staff records. He'd told us 'John is away and so I am in charge and I will not tolerate lateness if I see you off the phones I will want to know the reason why.'

I put Mrs. Grant on hold and called him over. 'Joe, could you speak to this very rude woman please she is demanding a manager and saying I am being rude. She wants a £5 voucher but she's already had several and the notes say not to issue her any more.'

Joe looked at me and said 'If I find you have been rude to her I will discipline you and you could get a written warning.'

I looked at him, mouth agape. The temporary manager thing had clearly gone to his head and if this was what he believed the role of team manager involved, he had a lot to learn. The minute he put my headset on his attitude changed. 'Hello Mrs Grant, Thank you so much for waiting there, I am so sorry to keep you waiting... How are you today? Yes... yes... OK... Oh, did she? Oh I see... I'm so sorry. Yes I will have a chat with her, of course she shouldn't have spoken to you like that please accept my apologies. No, of course we don't tolerate that type of attitude from staff. I am so sorry I will make sure she is dealt with. Tell you what Mrs Grant, I will send you a voucher for your trouble, no, tell you what, actually I'll send you two vouchers as an apology. Is that alright Mrs Grant? OK, OK, Mrs Grant - lovely to talk to you today - you take care now. Goodbye Mrs Grant, yes you too. Bye now.'

I had the urge to throw something large and heavy at him. He looked at me and said 'I'll be listening to that call and as I've said it could lead to a disciplinary for you.'

Thankfully he was never promoted and I received an apology.

That type of team leader was sadly all too common in the call centre, especially those with a high turnover of staff and where the managers were barely out of nappies. Some managers lacked spirit, passion, conviction, common sense, and in his case, appropriate dangly bits.

An abusive caller rang from the outer reaches of Scotland and refused to listen to anything I told him. We only delivered there twice a week. His payment had been rejected and so his order was not picked or delivered.

He rang and began hollering at me almost immediately. Apparently it was all my fault.

'If my payment doesn't go through then I will pay cash on delivery. For heaven's sake are you stupid?'

'No sir, I'm not stupid. We can't pick your order before it's paid for and we don't offer cash on delivery.'

'Right! I'm going to come down there personally; then you'll know what hit you. I know where you are and then you'll be sorry. I'm a big lad and I could smash your teeth right down your fucking throat with just one punch. Do you want that? Because I'll do it and don't think I won't…'

What a charmer! At a guess his house was over 400 miles from the office and we had two hours to closing.

He continued, '…so unless you want me to come and beat the crap out or you and your effing managers I suggest you get my food to me RIGHT NOW.'

I sighed; customers were so excitable sometimes. I let him vent on for a while until my manager, who was sitting behind me, asked if everything was OK. I signaled for him to listen in, which he did.

After a few further minutes of further blood-curdling threats, my manager had heard enough and jumped on to the line.

'Hello sir, My name's Jeremy, I'm the team manager and I've been listening in to the call…'

'Oh have you? Well then you'd better sort this bloody ridiculous issue out then, Jeremy, because if you don't, I'm going to come down there and punch your lights out.'

'Righto Sir,' Jeremy remained upbeat. 'I've just googled the distance from your address to our office and it is about 374 miles. I finish in two hours and I'll be in the car park at ten. I am the short guy with glasses and beard; bald head, wearing a blue shirt and tie. Would you like the address or would you like us to sort this out over the phone to save you the journey, which may be slightly more sensible may it not? I can see that you are scheduled for the first delivery slot in the morning anyway providing your card clears; that's if you're back home in time of course.'

Oddly enough the customer never turned up in the office car park, Jeremy and I went home unscathed and the customer had his shopping first thing the following morning, as he would have done whether he'd called or not.

Jeremy was perfect for a call centre. He seemed able to diffuse almost any situation with a customer. He told us his mother had always said he had the perfect face for a call centre.

12. The Birthday Present

The grocery call centre was hellishly busy around Christmas. One year in mid-December, at about 6pm, the call board was flashing neon red: 136 calls waiting. The longest had been there 37 minutes. I knew this, not because I was taking any notice of the damn board, but because a manic manager was leaping up and down shouting it at the top of his voice.

'Hello love,' said my customer, 'I'm sure you must be busy so I'll make it quick. You've sent me own brand Vodka but I only drink Smirnoff.'

'Oh, I'm so sorry about that, it looks like they ran out of the Smirnoff.'

'That's OK love, no problems, I haven't touched it. I was just wondering if I could keep it for the driver to swap when he comes on Thursday...' The customer was lovely.

'That shouldn't be a problem, I think I'll need some myself before the night is over,' I joked.

'Oh dear, luvvie,' she said. 'You must be busy so I won't keep you. I hope your night goes OK.'

'124 in the queue,' bellowed the manager, a foot from my ear.

'Who the devil was that?' the customer was clearly not impressed. 'What the hell is going on there?'

I felt I should apologise for the manager. 'I'm so sorry, he made me jump too, it's just that we're really busy right now and he wants the calls answered.'

The customer's mood turned; 'You listen to me,' she said, 'I'm your customer and you're dealing with me. Let me tell you I don't care if there are a thousand calls in your damn queue, I've waited almost an hour to get through to you and I will have my rightful attention.'

It was a well-known call centre phenomenon. While our callboards told us *exactly* how long to the second a customer had been waiting, the customers appeared to live in some kind of time warp. They always insisted they'd been waiting precisely twice as long as displayed on the callboard.

She wasn't happy and after yelling at me for the manager's 'downright rude behaviour', she demanded to speak with him herself, then and there, to give him her own ear bending.

As she refused to get off my phone until she had spoken with him and she was tying up my line, I had no option but to pass my headset to my manager and left him to it while I went to get us both a well-deserved cup of something hot.

At the end of some complaint calls customers often threw what they clearly believed to be the ultimate shocker, 'I'll never shop with you again. I'm going to your competitor.' I was never sure if they expected me to cry, beg and plead for them to stay or maybe offer them my firstborn child.

There was always an overwhelming temptation to say, 'That's great! Off you go you whinging old trout and I hope you have a very happy relationship with them; I won't lose an ounce of sleep over it and if I never have to speak with you again, I'll be more than happy.'

I had a call from a lady who was clearly angry

about something or other and when I tried to find her details I found no record of her or of any of her orders or accounts or anything at all. Further abuse followed about how incompetent I was, how ridiculous it was, how disgusted she was and so on.

Finally I asked her to read the very top of her receipt top to bottom; I had an inkling something was amiss. Sarcastically she said the first word at the top of the receipt, 'Sainsburys'.

'OK!' I said, as if a bolt of inspiration had hit me from above. 'Perhaps you should call Sainsburys then.'

A Eureka moment clearly hit the customer. 'I *have* rung, you're not... Oh for fu...' click.

She wasn't the first or the last.

Regularly, especially around Christmas, customers called ranting and raving about non-delivery of their order. They'd run through the usual speech about how they'd never trust us again and it was disgraceful and now their kids were condemned to starvation. They'd waited in for their order for hours and now they intended to tell the police/news/radio/MP/TV, whoever about us.

They'd try to get us to believe their whole life had been ruined due to our total incompetence and try to demand compensation. Finally, it would emerge the order had not been delivered because their payment had been rejected, usually because they'd given duff card details or simply because they didn't have enough money in their account.

I swear some thought we were a charity. One or two had the decency to apologise or sound sheepish, but most blamed us and we got an earful anyway.

Working in a modern call centre opened my eyes to people I never knew existed, people who I'd probably have crossed the street, even moved house to avoid. They were the type of people my mother warned me about and they appeared with alarming regularity on the other end of my phone.

Naturally I didn't get to choose which of these individuals I spoke to because they were force fed down my headset and I had to get used to it.

Some swore like crazy, which I found amusing. 'This bloody weather; it's rained for days now and the dog, the bloody silly, daft, bugger, has been rolling in the mud.' This was day-to-day-speak for many people and although the customer used naughty words, it clearly wasn't offensive.

Then there was 'You stupid f***ing idiot - you're bloody useless'. In that case it was aimed personally at the handler and did cause great offence.

Other customers could be offensive without swearing. My colleague, an ex-university maths lecturer of 32, with two kids and a PHD in applied mathematics, was told by a customer that as an owner of a business, a sandwich van as it turned out, he hadn't got time to speak with stupid telephone staff. He said she was clearly just a silly girl who clearly had no intelligence or concept of the real world or real people's needs.

Another caller I'd prefer to forget was a man complaining there wasn't a convenient Christmas delivery slot for him, which he described as, 'Bloody inconvenient'.

I did all the usual apologising. 'I'm so sorry, but the vans are extremely busy over Christmas and most people have booked weeks before, we do have a few slots left a few hours earlier in the day though.'

'I don't *want* an earlier slot, I *want* my regular slot, I shop with you every week and I *want* **my** slot.'

'I'm really sorry, but that slot has already been booked, what about the following day?'

'Listen to me girl, (yes, He called me *girl!*) I earn £11.62 an hour and I need to work, that's why I get my shopping delivered. Are YOU going to pay me £11.62 an hour to do my shopping?'

In their tiny little minds the customers truly believed they were being rational - bless!

Sadly customers very rarely called to say how happy they were, (although it did happen once; in June 1986, I believe).

***

On special occasions such as staff birthdays, there were always sugary delights to be enjoyed. The lucky ones were those whose team members clubbed together to buy cakes. The not so lucky ones had to buy the cakes themselves. At least once a week everyone was asked to chip in to somebody's birthday, wedding or leaving present, often someone they'd never even heard of.

Not wanting to appear to be a skinflint, most people chipped in, although in my experience, to get anything on your own birthday meant dropping hints at least five times a day every day for at least four weeks beforehand.

One of my managers was organised enough to keep a note of all our birthdays and that year my team presented me with a surprise birthday present; it was too small to contain the usual flowers or chocolates. Everyone gathered round, watching me intensely.

The tag on the outside said 'To help you deal with difficult customers'. I opened the tiny box to find a rag doll about five inches tall, on one side was a female doll's face, framed with long blonde hair. She was dressed in a tiny skirt and a little blue, flecked blouse. On the reverse was a man's face with a shirt, tie and trousers. There was also a small pouch with six blood-red headed, sharp pins inside…

The accompanying leaflet, translated into English, said it was a *stress doll*. It said if ever any person caused me stress or anger, I should use the doll accordingly and my stress would be magically taken away. There was also a warning that this was not a toy and *serious consequences could arise from incorrect usage.*

Feeling both grateful they had remembered my birthday and slightly apprehensive about the nature of the doll, I thanked them politely and put it in the very bottom of my workbox in case of future need.

Ten minutes before shift end, only days later, I took a call from a particularly rude and obnoxious oik demanding to speak to a manager. When I explained that, unfortunately, there wasn't one available that time of night, but I could get one to call him the following day, he told me I was f***ing useless and asked what was the point of me being there if I couldn't do the f***ing job?

His opinion was clear; I was completely stupid and how the f*** did I manage to get a job with an attitude like mine? I was apparently just an f***ing idiot minion who worked for a f***ing backstreet company. The usual obscenities spewed forth.

During his screaming tirade, I was trying to pack up my stuff in the vain hope I'd get away on time. As 10pm came and went and my team mates started to leave, I remembered the little doll in the little cloth bag. I reached for it and a sinister prickly feeling washed over me.

As I began to unwrap it, the little doll landed on my desk, man side up. Absent-mindedly I opened the pins and had a wicked urge to stick one in the doll's eye. My caller was still screaming away on the line, but I no longer heard him. I took the pin and stabbed and stabbed and then stabbed some more, all over the doll's body. It felt *good*. Some colleagues had realised that I was on a particularly bad call and come over to check I was OK.

They stared in mock horror as they saw me stabbing pins into the doll. I must admit it got a teeny bit frenzied. Finally I picked up the doll for one last stab, held it high in the air for effect and very deliberately, in front of everyone, stabbed it hard through the head...

...and felt a sharp pain, having stabbed right through the doll and into my finger. As the pain hit I dropped the doll, to my work mates' hoots of hysterical laughter. A bright red globule of blood appeared on my finger.

'You think it's' funny do you?' asked the voice on the phone. 'Right, I've got your name and I'll be complaining about you as well when your manager calls me tomorrow!' He hung up.

Laughter, being contagious, had spread to all six remaining staff who were now bent-double, hooting at me. They had tears rolling down their faces and I helplessly joined in, laughing until my sides hurt. All the stress had completely gone, replaced with laughter. The customer had gone, too, so I guess the doll had worked; although probably not in the way it was intended.

The tale was repeated to other colleagues over the next few weeks, although instead of a 'stress doll' it became "Izzy's Voodoo doll". I'm not particularly superstitious, but in retrospect I guess the stress doll was a form of black magic: perhaps the stabbed finger was a roundabout warning not to dabble in the supernatural: anyway, I never used the doll again and when I left the job I donated it to the team for use only in the direst of emergencies.

13. My Least Favourite Customer

Let me introduce some of the rudest customers I've ever had the misfortune to have been forced down my headset.

Sometimes the most minor issues provoked the worst calls. In the grocery delivery trade some customers appeared to believe their basic human rights had been breached because their shopping wasn't delivered on time or had an item missing.

Giving people access to a free, open-practically-all-hours helpline meant they often called when they were at the peak of their anger and while the steam was still hissing from their ears, rather than waiting for the line to open the next day after they'd calmed down.

The first such customer called late one January evening on a night when it was snowing heavily throughout the UK, all the delivery vans had been delayed and I was wondering how, or even if, I'd get home that night.

Her delivery, she said, was two hours late, so I rang the driver. As he didn't answer I checked with the store who informed me the driver had suffered a serious accident while on his delivery round due to the appalling road conditions and had been ambulanced to hospital. Consequently, there weren't going to be any deliveries from him that evening and possibly for a long time. The store manager was clearly having a bad night.

I clicked back to the customer, 'I am so sorry, our driver has had an accident and won't be able to get to you tonight. We can try to get another...'

'I don't give a f***ing TOSS if your driver

and his f***ing van is at the bottom of a f***ing cliff, that's not MY problem, it's yours. I want my f***ing shopping and I want it Now!' was her reply.

What a sweetheart!

The second customer unfortunately came though on my line about two hours before the end of my last shift before Christmas. I should have finished on a high; instead I went home extremely wound up, absolutely fuming and ready to put an axe through the head of the first person who upset me.

Training always taught us never to take calls personally, but some calls rapidly became horribly personal. This wretched evil witch of a woman was so awful, I was shaking when I ended the call. During my career I'd dealt with the general public thousands of times, but never had I spoken to anyone quite as rude as her.

Of course, battling with other shoppers also involved with the malarkey of Christmas is never a relaxing experience.

The brave roll up their sleeves, sharpen their elbows and head for the shops. This way they can pick and pack their own items, taking as much time as they like and when it's all done they can relax, knowing the hard work is done and their lovely family will have all they could want and need and lots more besides.

Of course shopping deliveries are essential for the elderly, infirm or disabled. They are also helpful for those with young families as shopping with young kids in tow can be a nightmare.

For most people though, having their groceries delivered is an option and perhaps even a luxury. It's *NOT a basic human right!*

Home delivery customers paid a small amount, sometimes nothing, for somebody else to pick and deliver their items so that they could do more important things such as watch TV, go to the pub or just sit on their lardy arses and do nothing. The amount paid (at the time £2 to £6) in no way covered the real cost of picking, storing and delivering the items.

The shopping-picker, often a student or young person in their first job, had a target to hit and hundreds of items to pick for many people at the same time. Errors were occasionally made, items were sometimes out of stock and alternatives weren't always available. Some food items had a shorter life than a customer may have picked themselves. Sometimes items were damaged in transit. These shortcomings were not deliberate.

On December 23rd at 20:37, our delivery driver had just dropped off a Christmas order to Mrs Farquhar. She checked the whole order, all was fine except the yoghurt, which was dated Boxing Day and *horror of horrors*, her cranberries were missing! Her entire Christmas was therefore going to be totally and utterly *ruined.*

She decided to phone us, the incompetent call-centre idiots and give us damn useless clowns a piece of her mind. When her family realized there'd be no cranberries at Christmas, they'd know she was a failure as a wife, a mother and a cook. Her whole *life* would simply no longer be worth living. We had clearly ruined her whole life. Oh boy were we damned imbeciles going to get a piece of her mind! How very dare we? She'd PAID (a whole £3.50) for the service and we'd made a mockery of her.

She punched the numbers into her phone, her pulse going like the clappers. Incompetent idiots, we were damn well going to pay for the mistake. Her heart beat loudly as she dialled… and got a busy message saying her call was in the queue and would be answered as soon as possible. Her blood pressure spiked even higher. The answerphone message repeated.

'We are very sorry to keep you waiting at this extremely busy time, however we know you are waiting and your call is important to us, please continue to hold and your call will be answered shortly.'

Her pulse-rate was now through the roof: we'd not only ruined her life but were going to be the cause of her early demise as well. Oh boy were we going to get it.

Finally, after eighteen minutes and thirty seven seconds, her call was answered by a 'smiling' voice, the owner of which was doing her utmost to sound friendly, still trying to smile though her face ached and her smiley voice was beginning to sound like a cheese grater.

The owner of that voice was me. I'd been in work for over six hours and still had another two to go. I'd already spoken to 47 other people that day only seven of which had had an ounce of Christmas spirit to offer.

Seventeen callers had already rung to complain that their shopping wasn't quite as perfect as it would have been had they got off their fat arses and gone to the store and picked it themselves.

The previous caller wanted compensation, because yoghurt had leaked over his bananas and he'd had to wash them. I could only imagine the trauma he'd suffered!

But this caller, no cranberries; the horror!

'Good evening, Thank you for calling, my name's Izzy. How can I help you today?'

'Right,   yourdriverhasdeliveredmyshopping... and I am DIS-GUSTED'.

Despite having many other people shouting and screaming abuse at me for the past six hours, I knew this customer should be treated with respect and as an individual. I was trained to be professional and polite. The customer was probably traumatised and upset. Perhaps something absolutely terrible had happened!

'Oh I'm sorry to hear that, let me take a look at this for you...'

'It's simply *not* good enough, my cranberries are missing. I'd ordered them for a reason you know, I was going to make cranberry sauce and now I have no cranberries, it is totally disgusting. What the hell am I going to do now for Christmas dinner? Huh - you tell me! It is simply not good enough! I want my cranberries delivered to me NOW!'

It was clearly toys out of the pram time.

'OK, let me just take your details and I'll see what I can do for you. Would you mind if I put you on hold a minute to see if I can contact the driver...'

'No you won't SEE if you can contact the driver you WILL contact the driver and you will do it NOW.'

'OK, I'll just see what I can do. I could offer you a refund if you prefer'.

'I DONT WANT A BLOODY REFUND,' she

said slowly and loudly as if she was talking to an imbecile, 'I want my bloody *cranberries*. You've obviously not been listening to me'

'OK, bear with me and I'll call the driver'.

I cleared her security and rang the driver. He didn't answer.

'Hello Mrs Farquhar. I'm very sorry, the driver doesn't appear to be answering. I think he may be driving. I can...'

'What do you mean he's not answering? That is not MY problem is it? It is YOUR problem and YOU are going to sort it out. I want YOU to get my cranberries to me NOW'

'OK Mrs Farquhar I'm really sorry about this but I need to contact the driver to see whether he has the items on the van and if so, whether he's able to return to you...'

'What do you mean 'IF'? No! You listen to me YOU WILL CONTACT THE DRIVER, you will do it now and I want my items in the next ten minutes this is absolutely disgusting, totally unacceptable, I'm absolutely *not* going to wait for your incompetence and hang on this phone. You will get my shopping to me and you will do it *now*. I don't want to hear your incompetent excuses'.

'Right Mrs Farquhar I'll see if I can contact the driver and call you back...'

'No you will NOT call me back - I'm very busy. I just want my items. How dare you tell me I can't have my shopping. How dare you tell me it is up to me to chase it. That's YOUR job and your effort to help me is abysmal. It is absolutely disgusting. I paid for a service how dare you tell me to deal with it'.

The crazy woman was mid-flow on a full

blown tantrum, clearly not listening or hearing. I'd let her vent but she showed no sign of slowing down.

I sat there feeling my blood pressure rising, knowing I had to remain professional and let her tirade of abuse to rise over my head. I was literally shaking with frustration and I felt sick.

Mine was a typical 'fight or flight' type reaction. In regular face to face life I'd have walked away, or run, a natural reaction when faced with a wild animal with teeth bared; either that or hit the animal very hard in the face with a stick. In my opinion, I was in a very similar situation, but without the ability to run and sadly with no stick.

Mrs Farquhar continued her verbal assault, telling me I only worked in a call centre and so obviously didn't understand the stresses and strains of someone with an important job. She inferred I was personally unimportant, incompetent, clearly stupid and lacking in intelligence, immature, extremely rude and boy, was she going to make me suffer for it.

I wasn't able to help myself... 'Mrs Farquhar is there any need to be quite so rude? I'm trying to help you!' I could have done with my stress doll and all six pins at that moment.

'Excuse ME! Just who do you think you are talking to? How DARE you call me rude! You've been extremely rude, incompetent and totally unhelpful. What's your name?'

'My name's Izzy.' I fought my urge to spell 'Izzy', tempting though it was.

'Well Izabelle, I assume that's short for Izabelle. I hope these calls are recorded. Are these calls recorded Izabelle? I hope they are, because Izabelle, I think you have been very rude and unhelpful and I'm going to complain about you, Izabelle. I'm sure your seniors will be interested to know how you speak to people Izabelle. I've noted the time and the date of this call and I am going to put in a complaint about *you* Izabelle'.

'Mrs Farquhar I've offered to help you and I've offered to call you back. I'm not able to do anything right now as I can't contact the driver. I need to contact him to see if he has your cranberries and if he does to see if he's able to return with them. Can I call you back?'

'I don't want you to call me back. I don't want to speak to you. You've been very rude, incompetent and unhelpful. I'm very busy and I don't want you to interfere with my evening any further than you already have. You've been extremely rude to me and I'm going to take this further. You get my items to me and you do it NOW! Goodbye!' She slammed down the phone.

I sat in my chair, my heart racing, literally shaking with emotion. I'd never speak to anyone the way that woman spoke to me. I wouldn't speak to a dog the way she spoke to me. I'd done all in my power to help the woman and still I had to listen to a tirade of abuse aimed at me personally. I was expected to remain professional and polite.

We were all told in our training that any abuse is not personal, but the constant use of my full first name was clearly intended as personal and was extremely condescending, as was the suggestion I was just a call centre worker, an incompetent one at that, who was both rude and stupid.

Of the 70-odd calls I was expected to take in a day and the 300 or 400 calls I took in a week that woman got right under my skin and really upset me. I was still shaking half an hour later when a burning hot tear rolled down my face. I'm not a kid, nor am I stupid and I was abused by this excuse for humanity, albeit verbally.

I wondered if the woman would complain about me. If she did, would the company back me up or give me a warning? I replayed the call over and over in my head; all I did was to ask the customer if it was really necessary to be quite so rude. Of course I knew all calls were recorded and this customer would probably call back to complain about me.

I wanted to scream, to cry, or just talk it over with someone. I felt sick; after two years at that call centre only two or three customers had affected me that badly. I put my phone code in 'emergency break' and went to get myself and my friend Jo a nice cup of tea. I had eight minutes total available to use but had used two of them earlier to get a coffee.

When I returned with the teas, I was still shaking. The job was definitely affecting my health. I tried to tell Jo about the call. She was sympathetic having had many similar calls herself. Everyone on the team was familiar with them.

Jo asked if I was OK - I wasn't, I was still shaking. What I needed was a shooting range or a punch-bag or a stiff whisky. However, my emergency break of six remaining minutes had finished and I had another 67 minutes to go before I could go home.

I put my headset back on, plugged myself back into Hell, and clicked my phone into 'ready' - there was a long queue of calls waiting. 'BEEP,' and on with the next one.

I officially finished my shift at 9.30 that night

although I wasn't able to go home until 9.47 as I had to finish dealing with another complaint before I left.

I have no idea if Mrs Farquhar called back. I had done all I could and I certainly wasn't going to attempt to 'go the extra mile' for her. I knew, other than refunding the damn cranberries there was nothing I could have done and I certainly wasn't going to call her back. Perhaps she called again and another colleague told her where to stick her cranberries.

When I finally got home my husband and the kids were all in bed and fast asleep so I had no one to talk to. I was still upset, with a tight knot in my stomach which stubbornly refused to untie for days.

Those types of call used to fester in my head unless I could talk about them to somebody who understood. The other way of letting go was to write it down as soon as possible. I did exactly that and you have just read the exact transcript, word for word.

If we ever tried to discuss such calls with colleagues our rants were usually interrupted with 'Good evening, thank you for calling…' as another call came in and the colleague switched attention to the call. We were left talking to thin air with a millisecond to wrap up our story in mime.

Friends and family who'd never experienced a call centre didn't understand so calls grew in my head like a tapeworm until they consumed my very being. They woke me at night, and if I was unlucky enough to take a bad call last thing on a Friday they ruined my weekend as well.

I always thought of all manner of wild, witty and wonderful retorts I could have given on the call if only I'd thought of them at the time.

Occasionally a caller, clearly bored or with some bug to bear, deliberately rang with no other aim than to prove what sad little people some of them were.

Although we were based in the UK, we were told to avoid wishing customers 'Merry Christmas' in the misguided belief we may have offended someone of a different faith.

Everyone in the centre wished each other a happy whatever occasion they were celebrating. I saw no reason why it should have caused offence to anyone. Sometimes though, a 'Happy Christmas' just slipped out at the end of a conversation with a customer;

Me: 'Is there anything else I can help you with today?'

Customer: 'No, that's it, thanks.'

Me: 'Thanks for calling and Merry Christmas.' The minute I'd said it I bit my tongue, hoping this wasn't one of those very few customers who may have been offended and hoping even if it wasn't, that it wouldn't be a monitored call.

Customer: (with a change of tone) 'What did you just say?'

Me: 'Thank you for calling…'

Customer: 'Don't you dare! You said *Merry Christmas*! I'm an atheist! Do you realise how offended I am?'

Me: 'I'm sorry. I didn't mean to offend you.'

Customer: 'Get me your supervisor, NOW!' I slunk over to a manager somewhat sheepishly to explain. She rolled her eyes when I gave the customer's name. 'Oh is that so? Right! Pass him to me!' She seemed more than willing to take the call. 'Thank you for holding, sir. My colleague explained to me what happened and I'm really sorry if you were offended in any way.'

Customer: 'What kind of stupid people do you have working there? I'm an atheist, why on earth would she wish me Merry Christmas? I'm deeply offended.'

Supervisor: 'Again, sir, I do apologise if you were offended, but you know I don't celebrate Christmas either and I'm not creating a fuss about people wishing me a Merry Christmas! I can also see from your notes you have called nine times already today. Did you actually want something this time or was it another social call?'

After the customer hung up she told me the same man had called several times that day for something trivial and it appeared likely he was doing it specifically to provoke that reaction in an attempt to extract compensation.

14. Same Old, Same Old

Many features of the job of call handler were the same in all the call centres I worked in. My very least favourite call centre aspects were;

1)   Getting stuck on the phones at break or home time was an everyday occurrence for call handlers and was usually unpaid. Leaving on time was an acquired skill which I never mastered so I frequently worked up to half an hour after my scheduled finish time.

2)   Having to give my full name on every call: Some centres allowed us to only give our first name and staff number, others thought it more professional to give our full name. The only issue we had was that with modern technology, those of us with unusual names could be traced on social media by any dubious customer who wished to do so. It happened a few times to colleagues.

3)   Having to ask 'Is there anything else I can help with?' on every call. It was apparently good customer service; although it regularly backfired badly, especially on complaint calls where the customer predictably replied that as we hadn't bloody helped in the first place we were now just taking the mickey. I lost count of how often the customers asked for the lottery numbers as if they were the first to think of such a hilarious question.

4)   The cursed desk. One desk in every centre was guaranteed to feed its occupant calls direct from hell all evening. Usually this was the desk I was sitting at.

5)   Lack of staff psychic training; when a customer rang, we were expected to know their entire history immediately, together with all details of their account and every detail of any conversation they'd ever had with us. A customer rang late one evening to say one of our vans had nearly run her off the road and she wanted the driver's name to make a complaint. I asked for the van registration number, she didn't have it. Did she have the description of the driver? 'No, it was bloody dark'. What road was she on? She didn't know she was on holiday, but she was in Wales. What time did it happen? 'Yesterday evening sometime after six'.

6)   Air Conditioning. When one person got a bug, the air conditioning was guaranteed to ensure it was evenly distributed throughout the entire office within hours.

7)   The office coffee machine. This was cleaned on a Monday and it wasn't until Wednesday afternoon it stopped tasting of anti-bac spray.

Good things also happened in the call centre;

1)   Fire alarm: This was always a *drop everything and go* scenario. Fire drills were regularly practiced so staff calmly walked outside to the designated spot in the car park. It was a rare opportunity to have a chat with colleagues, a sly ciggie and a few minutes off the phone. No matter how many times we said we had to go, customers never accepted the urgency, despite the alarms wailing in the background. It was the only time we could hang up on them.

2)   One to one meetings with the manager: at least half an hour off the phones. If we were clever it was possible to stretch it out for a whole hour by engaging the manager in a deep and meaningful conversation, although it was pointless if the phones were busy.

3)   Ongoing Training Films: Training updates, new procedures and systems all offered time off the phone for a relaxed uninterrupted chat with colleagues. Again, if the phones were busy, training was the first thing pulled, often at very short notice.

4)   The phone system crashed: This was the topping on the cake as it could last for hours. When the phones went down there was nothing we could do other than catch up on emails or one-to-one preparation. Sadly when the phones were subsequently fixed, the customers came through in large numbers, all

wanting to whinge because they'd been unable to get through earlier on.

5) Wrong number: 'Oh, I'm sorry, I've called the wrong number.' Excellent call if it was the end of the day because the call handler went to the back of the call queue and occasionally even meant they could go home on time.

6) Prank callers: These were usually obvious from the beginning. Usually there was a lot of giggling in the background, the caller was often slurring as if on either drink or drugs, or they ignored the greeting entirely, launching directly into their hilarious (not) call.

7) Some of the ones I had;
'Do you sell horse burgers like other stores?'
'What are you wearing?'
'Do you sell flavoured condoms?'
'I am a vampire and I need to drink blood.'
'My Tena-lady has leaked.' (a male caller).
'There's a giraffe in my lettuce.'
'Are your eggs from white or brown chickens?'
Man 'I bought some ladies knickers but they don't fit me, can I bring them back?'
'F***, Bo*****s, T***, C*** you're a W*****' followed by riotous laughter and a click of the receiver.

Most prank calls were about as amusing as toothache and sometimes we didn't even get to hear the punchline due to loud sniggering in the background. One or two people thought it funny to spew forth as many obscenities as they could muster in the time they had before we hung up. Some tried to goad us into swearing back.

There was always that little niggling thought in the back of my head; what if this was a genuine call and the caller had mental issues and had genuinely needed help?

Most of the time I let them carry on, sometimes even playing along and pretending to take them seriously. This method tended to deflate their delicate little egos and they often became confused as the call was no longer funny. The longer they were tying up my phone line, the less time I had to spend on people who were serious about throwing abuse at me.

15. My Final Call Centre

After working at the grocery call centre for two years, two months and two days too many, Jo and I got to the stage where every day was a struggle to stay sane. Battling the urge to take in an AK47 and use it, we both began looking for a new job, figuring there had to be more to life. Anything had to be better.

Weeks later I came up trumps. I saw a temporary job advertised in the financial industry and hoping I'd find a similar atmosphere to the one I'd been made redundant from previously, I applied.

Unfortunately it was another call centre but I weighed up my options and abandoned ship, leaving poor Jo behind in the grocery company.

The new call centre dealt with loans and credit cards. It was much better because there were fewer calls, although each call was longer and a lot more in depth. As a financial company, there was a lot more training and knowledge required for the job.

On the positive side the customers gave the staff a lot more respect and usually rang when they had time and were in the right frame of mind. Because most customers wanted to borrow money, they appeared to believe by being nice they had a better chance of a positive outcome.

There were still customers who shouted and swore and threw their toys out of the pram but the rules were far less flexible and the answers more consistent. All figures were put in the computer and if the computer said *no*, that was the end of it.

Most of the staff at the financial company were lovely, more mature, and mostly great fun as well. Although far more professional than the grocery company, they also knew how to enjoy themselves. The dress code was casual smart with a dress down each Friday.

My team leader managed to balance professionalism along with being a bit of a goof with a bawdy sense of humour. The team members were nice enough although I never felt I knew them properly. Again, the busy call centre didn't allow much time for socialising.

My job was to take the customer's personal and financial details, following company and legal procedures, to establish whether they qualified for a loan. If they did then they were passed to an adviser to proceed to the next step.

It was amazing how many people called to discuss their personal finances while clearly driving up a very busy road: they may have had hands free but I couldn't see how it could be possible to make large financial decisions and concentrate seriously on what was being said while driving.

People also often called for very large loans with screaming babies and toddlers, dogs barking or the TV blaring in the background. I could barely hear myself think on some calls.

Because it was a financial company, training was ongoing to keep up with the strict regulations. Each day we each had thirty to forty emails, some were important, some were very important and some were vital financial regulation updates; others were to let us know the sandwich man was on site.

We had to try to read them all in between calls because we were logged in from the minute we started work. On a good day there was up to a minute between calls. Each call could take between five and twenty minutes or longer. There was the usual online training and preparation for 1-2-1's to do in between calls.

My problem was that as a part timer I worked core hours 9-4, whereas the rest of the team was on full time shift work doing anything from 8am to 9pm. Core hours were always busy and although occasionally there were four or five minutes between calls this wasn't sufficient to read all the emails.

Often I'd be ploughing through an email when a new call would come in. My train of thought was then lost in order to concentrate on the customer. After each call individual customer notes had to be updated and the email was forgotten.

Inevitably I missed important updates.

We were all strictly monitored to ensure we were giving the correct information at all times. There were scripts to be read verbatim on some calls while others required different tactics. Many customers asked questions which we didn't know the answers to so we had to go to an online manual of thousands of pages to find the correct answers. We weren't allowed to check with colleagues in case the answers had changed recently.

Looking up the answers took a lot of time and each call was monitored closely for AHT and hold time. If the customer was put on hold too long we were pulled up on it. If we gave the wrong answer we were given a warning and told to check the right answer and call the customer back. It was a black and white job in a multi-shaded world of grey.

Our AHT was checked regularly and if we

spent too long on a call we were challenged. Several calls each were monitored daily and warnings dished out for incorrect information given to a customer. Along with the mountains of work to be done in between calls when calls were back, I began to suffer symptoms of stress.

My stomach tied itself in a knot the moment I walked through the door and my heart raced as soon as I had the first bleep in my ear.

It was while I was working at this job that I woke up and wrote my list of reasons not to go to work on Monday morning.

And since I left I have never been tempted back, nor have I had any regrets.

Not ever!

One of the most common statements made in coffee breaks was, 'On my last day I'm going to tell the customers *exactly* what I think of them.'

This rarely happened because of another call centre quirk. On the last day all the customers were usually the sweetest, most polite and most grateful customers ever. My final customer ever involved the use of Big Red which was appropriately final.

I just saw an article on the local news. I think it sums up very nicely.

A man, working in a call centre in the city centre, was arrested and given the Don't Come Monday award. His was a stellar example of what can happen if you have a particularly bad day at the call centre. Colleagues countrywide were sniggering behind their monitors as the news got out and were having a huge laugh about it on social media.

Apparently a fellow call centre worker, who had been to the pub for a few lunchtime bevvies, reached snapping point one afternoon, and then, was taken just a little bit further.

He snapped, with true style and panache.

The papers didn't think it necessary to report the reason for the incident. I heard he had been asked to take an escalation from a colleague which he didn't want to take. Who could blame him?

He stood up in the middle of the call centre and began shouting, 'F*** you, F*** this and F*** the company.' With this he picked up several pieces of desk furniture and monitors and threw them around the office, accidentally hitting a colleague on the head, damaging a wall and £15,000 worth of computers.

He kicked the wall and went on a final rampage through the office swiping things off desks and shouting. He then walked out of the building shouting a few more choice obscenities as he went. When he got outside he punched a policeman who happened to be in the street after trying to talk a man down from the roof of the multi-storey car park opposite. (I don't know if he also worked in the call centre!)

Our hero was last seen in the back of the police van looking a little sheepish albeit apparently relieved he wasn't back in the call centre.

Welcome to the call centre world. Well done mate, surprised it wasn't me - almost been there, many times.

Bravo!

16. Different Levels of Stupid

Friends and colleagues have shared some of their experiences with me. It's good to know I'm not the only one who has suffered the Call Centre Experience.

There are many levels of stupid and I have included some of the calls which have reached the top. Sometimes I wonder how some people even manage to use a telephone.

One morning KJ, who worked in the travel insurance department, had a call from a young man who was intending to go on a gap-year backpacking adventure.

KJ: 'Can I start with your name and date of birth please?'

Caller: 'Uhhhhh,' there was a pause as he held the phone away from his ear, 'MUUUM! What's my date of birth?' A voice in the background shouted his date of birth which he relayed over the phone.

KJ: 'Okay, and what countries are you planning to visit?' The young man ran through a list of countries, starting in Europe then over to Asia, India, China and Japan and finally a road trip through America and then back to the UK.

KJ: 'Wow! That sounds exciting. Do you have any pre-existing medical conditions?'

Caller: 'Uhhhhhh.' Another pause, 'Muuuum! Do I have any pre-sisting medical conditions…?' After a pause KJ heard his mum shout back 'Yes! You have Diabetes and Asthma!'

Caller: 'Really? I have Diabetes?'

Mother: Now near the phone 'Yes! - What did you think your injections were for?'

Caller: 'Ooooooh! So that's what they're for!'

KJ: Stunned Silence. The young man accepted the quote after a few more questions and took out the policy. KJ hung up the phone and looked at her colleague on the next desk who'd been able to hear the whole conversation as the office was quiet.

Colleague: 'Fifty quid says that kid will wake up in a bathtub with his kidneys missing by day three.'

A call to a cable call centre; 'My phone modem has burned through several handsets and smells like it's on fire. Should I unplug it?'

CJ worked for a credit card company.

CJ: 'Hi, you're through to CJ. How I can help?'

Customer: 'I'm really, really cross about this!'

CJ: 'I'm sorry to hear that. How can I help?'

Customer: 'Well, frankly, I simply don't understand how you can justify this! You've ruined my day completely!'

CJ: 'Okay, how can I help?

Customer: 'Well, like I said, I don't understand. I spent all the money on the credit card you sent me and I told you I cut it up, so why the hell have you sent me a bill for it?'

CJ: 'You do realize that this is money you have borrowed from the bank? It's not free money!'

Customer: 'Why should I have to pay? I cut it up!'

CJ: 'It's still an amount you've borrowed from the bank which needs to be repaid. Just because you threw away the card, it doesn't cancel the debt!' CJ made several attempts to explain that the customer had to pay but the customer was having none of it.

Customer: 'But I can't I afford that. It's ridiculous. You people didn't make aware of this! I thought it all ended if I just cut up the card. I shouldn't have to pay this if I don't have the card! I want to make a complaint.'

CJ: 'Hold the line. I'll put you through…'

KJ worked for a bank.

KJ: 'Good afternoon, you're through to KJ. Do you have a policy number?'

The caller gave a policy number.

KJ: 'Thank you, now, can I take your name?'

Woman: 'Jane Smith.' It matched the account name.

KJ: 'Thank you. For security I just need to ask you a few questions. Can you tell me the first line of your address, the postcode and your date of birth?'

The woman gave all the details correctly.

KJ: 'Thank you, now how may I help you?'

Woman: 'I need to know what payments I've made on my account.'

KJ: 'I'll just check.' She went through all the payments with dates and amounts.

Woman: 'I'm going to have you arrested.'

KJ: 'Sorry, what…?''

Woman: 'You just breached the Data Protection Act. I'm not Jane Smith.'

KJ: 'Sorry …? If you're not Jane Smith then what is your name?'

Woman: (very smugly), 'Ann Gibbons. Put me through to your manager; I'm going to have you prosecuted. You can't just give away my friend's data like that.'

KJ: 'I see. Unfortunately, I think you'll find I have complied with the Data Protection Act. You, however, have committed fraud.'

Woman: 'No I haven't.'

KJ: 'I asked for your name. You said it was Jane Smith. You didn't say you were calling on her behalf – you said you *were* Jane Smith.'

Woman: 'No, you misheard; that's your fault!'

KJ: 'This call is recorded. We may need to report your fraudulent attempt to the police.'

Woman: 'Ha! Good luck finding me; you don't even know my name!'

KJ: 'Ann Gibbons?'

Woman: 'What? How did you know my name?'

KJ: 'You told me.'

Woman: 'No I didn't. You're lying!'

KJ: All our calls are recorded…

Click…

The following are things I have heard during my own call centre years and some are from friends who have shared some of their own customer quotes with me;

Customer of a financial company following an admin charge for a third missed monthly payment;

'I can't afford a £10 fee, I'm going on a cruise next week and just forked out for a new i-phone.'

Customer of the grocery company: 'I'm NEVER giving my business to you ever again. I am going to your competitor. So what do you say to that?'

Staff: 'Bye then.'

A cable TV customer who received a fine for two missed payments: 'I can't afford it, my husband has recently died and I had to pay for the funeral!' Badly acted tears followed.

Staff: 'I'm so sorry to hear that. If you could please send the death certificate in we'll close the account without a fee.'

Customer: 'Are you calling me a liar? How dare you call me a liar when I'm in such an emotional state. Why would I make such a thing up?'

The *deceased* husband called a week later to complain about the fine.

Personal loan customer, after missing another payment; 'It's absolutely ridiculous you're charging me for only the third missed payment in a row. I'm going to report you to the Omnibus.'

Customer who had called her bank; 'I don't want to confirm my personal details to you. How do I know you're not scamming me?'

Staff; 'Er, *you* called *us*.'

Customer of a large TV and internet provider; 'I can't pay these fees any more, I have five children and a huge mortgage. I have loan repayments to make and my husband has left me. You have to help me. I'm paying you far too much.'

Staff: 'Of course, let's see; you're on the top package at the moment with access to all channels. We could save you up to £40 a month if you reduced to the basic package with just the basic channels.

Customer; 'What? No way! You're suggesting I cut out those extra channels; don't be ridiculous. Can't you just reduce the price? I need help not my luxuries being taken from me.'

TV package Customer; 'You've taken £1.37 extra

from my account and you'd damn well better have a good reason for doing it. Come on; what's your excuse this time?

Staff; 'Ah that's the annual adjustment amount which we told you about last time you called and we also confirmed in writing.'

Customer; 'Well because of you I've now gone overdrawn causing me huge inconvenience and bank charges. What are you going to do about it?'

Staff; 'Madam, it is part of your annual payment to us, there is nothing we can do about it as you have signed the contract in agreement.'

Customer; 'You're nothing but thieves and you've stolen my money. I'm going to speak to my solicitor and tell the papers about this. I'll see you in court.'

Apparently she believed it would be cheaper to consult a solicitor than pay £1.37 she'd agreed to.

There are thousands of call centre workers in the UK and abroad who put up with these conversations on a daily basis. While most customers call because they genuinely need help, there will always be many others who are a challenge, whether it's down to ignorance, stupidity or just plain boredom.

To those of you poor tortured souls currently working in call centres worldwide, my thoughts are with you. I know what you're going through. You all deserve a medal.

As for me, now this book is finished, I'm going to find myself a nice little job somewhere quiet and stress free. As yet I have no idea where but one thing is for sure; It won't be in a call centre.

Take care out there; it's a crazy world!

Also by Izabelle Winter

'Diary of a Hoarder's Daughter'.

If you have seen *Hoarders* on TV, you may wonder what it's *really* like to grow up in a hoarded house.

After being taken to hospital with a broken back, my 82 year old father was told he couldn't go back home until his house was safe and free from any obstruction. He had to be able to move about freely.

This was virtually impossible with the house as it was because he was an extreme hoarder. His daughter was the only one able to step up for this task although she also had a young family on school summer break and a job and nightly visits to her father in hospital. As if this wasn't a big enough task, her father was adamant *nothing* was allowed to be thrown away.

As her narcissistic father lies in his hospital bed demanding to be released, Izabelle spends up to eight hours every day at the house and discovers lots of childhood memories which perhaps would have been better left uncovered including the possible reason for her mother's premature death.

Read why the Christmas lights were up in July. Discover how long a tin of tomatoes can be kept before it explodes. Why does a man with two feet need 173 shoes?

Many years after I moved out, fate forced me to return to re-live the childhood which I'd once considered normal. With fresh eyes I discover some things which should have stayed buried and a few shocking truths about my own childhood.

Author's Notes

If you have enjoyed this book, *please* be kind enough to take a minute to leave a review on Amazon. Each review is very much appreciated and I assure you I read each and every one.

If you'd like to ask me a question regarding either book you can contact me via my Facebook page. I will do my best to answer each and every question.

I also have a blog www.izabellewinter.blogspot.co.uk

Printed in Poland
by Amazon Fulfillment
Poland Sp. z o.o., Wrocław

51799668R00101